# *SUPER*FOODS
## COOKBOOK

**Michelle Bridges** has worked in the health and fitness industry for over 20 years as a professional trainer and group fitness instructor. Her key role in Network Ten's hit series *The Biggest Loser* and her highly successful online exercise and mindset program, the 12 Week Body Transformation, have connected her with hundreds of thousands of Australians, making her this country's most recognised and influential health and fitness expert. *Superfoods Cookbook* is her ninth book. Her previous books – *Crunch Time*, *Crunch Time Cookbook*, *Losing the Last 5 Kilos*, *5 Minutes a Day*, *The No Excuses Cookbook*, *Everyday Weight Loss*, *Your Best Body* and *Get Real!* – are all bestsellers.

# SUPERFOODS
## COOKBOOK

The facts, the foods and the recipes –
feel great, get fit and lose weight

## michelle bridges

VIKING
*an imprint of*
PENGUIN BOOKS

VIKING

Published by the Penguin Group
Penguin Group (Australia)
707 Collins Street, Melbourne, Victoria 3008, Australia
(a division of Penguin Australia Pty Ltd)
Penguin Group (USA) Inc.
375 Hudson Street, New York, New York 10014, USA
Penguin Group (Canada)
90 Eglinton Avenue East, Suite 700, Toronto, Canada ON M4P 2Y3
(a division of Penguin Canada Books Inc.)
Penguin Books Ltd
80 Strand, London WC2R 0RL England
Penguin Ireland
25 St Stephen's Green, Dublin 2, Ireland
(a division of Penguin Books Ltd)
Penguin Books India Pvt Ltd
11 Community Centre, Panchsheel Park, New Delhi 110 017, India
Penguin Group (NZ)
67 Apollo Drive, Rosedale, Auckland 0632, New Zealand
(a division of Penguin New Zealand Pty Ltd)
Penguin Books (South Africa) (Pty) Ltd
Rosebank Office Park, Block D, 181 Jan Smuts Avenue, Parktown North, Johannesburg 2196, South Africa
Penguin (Beijing) Ltd
7F, Tower B, Jiaming Center, 27 East Third Ring Road North, Chaoyang District, Beijing 100020, China

Penguin Books Ltd, Registered Offices: 80 Strand, London WC2R 0RL, England

First published by Penguin Group (Australia), 2014

10 9 8 7 6 5 4 3 2 1

Cover and text design by Adam Laszczuk © Penguin Group (Australia)
Cover and author photographs by Henryk Lobaczewski
Food photography by Julie Renouf, home economy by Caroline Jones, food styling by Georgia Young, photographer's assistant Linda Oliveri
Food consultant Lucy Nunes
Typeset in Frutiger & Geometric Slabserif by Adam Laszczuk © Penguin Group (Australia)
Colour reproduction by Splitting Image, Clayton, Victoria
Printed and bound in China by South China Printing Co Ltd

National Library of Australia
Cataloguing-in-Publication data:

Bridges, Michelle.
Superfoods cookbook: the facts, the foods and the recipes –
feel great, get fit and lose weight / Michelle Bridges.
ISBN: 9780670077762 (paperback)
1. Reducing diets--Recipes. 2. Cooking. 3. Wellbeing.

641.563

penguin.com.au

While every care has been taken in researching and compiling the dietary and exercise information in this book, it is in no way intended to replace or supersede professional medical advice. Neither the author nor the publisher may be held responsible for any action or claim howsoever resulting from the use of this book or any information contained in it. Readers must obtain their own professional medical advice before relying on or otherwise making use of the dietary and exercise information in this book.

# Contents

# *SUPER*foods introduction

These are my choices of the **superheroes of the food world**. These are the ingredients that really pack a punch in terms of their nutritional content. Incorporated into a healthy, balanced diet, they will help you lose weight, fight disease, increase wellbeing and train more effectively.

I've selected a range of ingredients from meat and fish to vegetables, fruit, nuts and grains that I feel should be on everyone's table. Their benefits range from boosting the functioning of your brain and helping your cells fight off infection to getting rid of toxins in your body and decreasing inflammation. **But these foods are not magical, mythical entities – they are everyday foods that just happen to be superstars in their field.**

Nutrients are not the only criterion by which foods get onto my list. They have to fulfill a few more requirements before they can be classed as 'super'.

Above all, they have to be easily available. I don't want to have to go to Tibet, climb a mountain and wait until the full moon rises to be able to get an ingredient. It's got to be at the market or the supermarket and on hand most of the time. Of course, there are caveats to that. For instance, there are times when fruit and vegetables are in season and so are at their most nutritious and taste their best. And, of course, there are questions of ethics and sustainability that need to be addressed when it comes to the meat and fish that we eat, but I will guide you through them. However, essentially, a superfood has to be readily at hand.

Secondly, a superfood can't break the bank. If you've got to fork over a whole paycheck just to get your hands on a few grams, it's not getting on my list. Most of the ingredients here cost no more than a few dollars, and often a lot less. When something is a bit more expensive, you either don't need so much of it, or you can use some and keep the rest in your pantry or fridge. And remember, when vegetables and fruits are in season – and at their best – they are also at their cheapest!

These foods are full of nutrients, packed with flavour, readily available and great value for money.

Superfoods alone won't get you to your goals, but they are a valuable addition to a healthy diet and regular exercise regime.

What's more, for a food to make my superhero list, the nutritional content has to be delivered effectively. By that, I mean that you shouldn't have to eat a barrel-full to get the benefit and there shouldn't be any hidden kicker that is detrimental even if you are getting nutrients along the way. One of the keys to ensuring the good always outweighs the bad is correct portion size. Take nuts, for example. They have many nutritional benefits but they are also pretty high in fat. So, we just use a few of them and take their calorie content into account when making a meal, combining them with lower-calorie ingredients to get a rounded, healthy dish.

This is one of the guiding principles behind the recipes in this book. They don't always have the superfood front and centre, but all of them are low-calorie, nutrient-rich dishes that combine flavourful ingredients to make meals that taste great while giving you a range of nourishing elements. I'm not gonna tell you to eat these superfoods and just munch down anything else you like – it doesn't work like that! **A healthy, balanced diet, rich in wholefoods and with correct portion (and ingredient) sizes is the way to go. All the ingredients in these recipes are good for you – the superfoods are just the ones that stand out from the pack a little more.**

Of course, everyday healthy eating is the way to reach your diet and fitness goals. A balanced diet that is high in wholefoods, predominantly comprising fruits, vegetables, protein and grains, and that keeps processed foods, alcohol and takeaway meals to a minimum, will get you where you want to go, whether that be losing weight, getting fitter or improving your general wellbeing. Add superfoods to that program and you are getting a nutritional boost right from the off.

**What we eat has a huge impact on the effectiveness of our training. Getting the right nutrients can help with preparation, performance and recovery when it comes to exercise.** The right diet can help to build muscle, ensure effective blood flow and heart function, limit inflammation, and, of course, give us energy to perform at our optimum level.

Our diet, as we know, also affects how much weight we put on or lose, and how effectively we maintain our desired weight. **Diet is the number one most important factor in weight loss.** With all the training in the world, if you eat crap, you are going to put on weight. Eating the right foods in the right amounts will mean you lose weight. My superfoods will help you do that.

Besides having an impact on our training and weight loss, the food we eat, and particularly superfoods, have other important things to contribute to our health and wellbeing. Certain nutrients can help us to ward off disease, live longer lives, boost our cognitive power, ensure the optimal operation of our physiological functions and even improve our mood.

We can be guilty of thinking that it is just 'bad' foods that affect our moods or our energy levels. 'I need a coffee to get me going in the morning,' 'A chocolate bar makes me feel happier.' We've all said these or similar things. But, in fact, a regular, healthy diet gives you these things and more, without, crucially, the calories or sugars unhealthy snacks invariably contain, and without the inevitable crash that comes when the short-term effects of such quick pick-me-ups wear off. These superfoods are so loaded with vitamins, minerals and other goodies that they provide you with energy for longer, meaning you are able to take more control over your food intake rather than looking for quick fixes.

**The other thing we shouldn't forget about my superfoods is . . . they are so goddamn tasty!** That's another criterion that meant these foods made the list. No one wants to eat something that tastes bad, even if they know it's good for them. I've chosen a wide variety of ingredients that offer a range of flavours, textures and possibilities for using them. None of these foods are just a one-dish wonder; they can all be used in different kinds of recipes. Take fruit, for example. The ones I've selected make handy snacks and add a lovely sweetness to a number of breakfasts, but I also use certain fruits in salads and to accompany grilled meat.

**Having these superfoods in your home opens a whole world of taste sensations.** Combined with their potent power on the nutrient front, they are real 'must-haves' in any kitchen.

Incorporating these superfoods into your meals is a great opportunity to expand and experiment with your cooking skills.

# *SUPER*foods & training

Superfoods can help give you energy, develop muscle, aid recovery and keep your body functioning well.

What you eat effects how well your body performs. This is true in terms of how much weight it stores, how good it is at fighting off infection and disease, and how well your metabolic and physiological processes function. But all those things are also affected by the amount of exercise you do. And your exercise, in turn, is affected by what you eat. Food, then, is the key to healthy living.

**The foods you eat can have a significant impact on how well you train, your energy levels and even your body's speed of recovery from its exertions.**

One of the key 'ingredients' in terms of your exercise abilities is the amount of lean muscle you have. Whether you are doing cardio or strength training, increasing your muscle mass while decreasing your percentage of fat will help you perform better, look better and feel better. **One of the primary components of muscle is protein. So it makes sense for protein to comprise a decent proportion of your diet.** The chemical elements in protein-rich foods help your muscles grow and strengthen. Fish is a good source of protein as it is delivered in a low-calorie form. While red meats such as beef also provide protein, they tend to have a higher fat content. Lean meats like my favourites, kangaroo and calves' liver, give you more benefit with less fat.

But there are other ways to get protein in your diet. Brussels sprouts, for instance, are full of the stuff, as is wheatgerm. So adding wheatgerm to your morning smoothie (rather than brussels sprouts!) before a workout is an effective way of helping your muscles perform well.

But the protein performance doesn't stop there. Add a few almonds into the mix and you are getting a good dose of zinc. Given that zinc helps your muscles to synthesise the protein you are taking in, your training performance and its results are stepped up again.

Of course, you don't want to be having a full fish dinner right before you go for a run. You'll feel uncomfortable with the food in your system. And besides, until the food gets into your intestines, the nutrients are not really absorbed. The amount of time it takes for food nutrients to be absorbed by your body varies, depending on the type of nutrient. For instance, sugars are absorbed much more quickly than fats (which is why you get an energy 'rush' when you have a sugary snack or fizzy drink), while proteins are somewhere in between. Generally, you should aim for eating an hour or two before you train. This allows your food to move to the intestines, the nutrients to begin being absorbed by your system, and for you to have gained some of the energy in the food.

Now, if you're like me and prefer to train first thing in the morning, eating beforehand is not really possible (I'm not suggesting you get up at 4 a.m., cook a meal then wait till 6 to go running). However, the slowing of your system during sleep means that you will still get some nutritional benefit from your meal the previous evening to help your training. I tend to have an apple or a banana before I train in the morning. Fruits like these give you an energy boost as they contain rapidly absorbed sugars, namely fructose, the natural form that is a lot better for you than the chemically manufactured and adulterated sucrose you find in processed and pre-packed snacks.

**Anti-inflammatory elements are also the exerciser's friend.** When you train you are putting your body under a certain amount of pressure and strain. By doing this you are forcing it to react, to become stronger, leaner and faster in response to what you are asking of it. Which is why you can feel a little achy after a session in the gym and tired after a run. Anti-inflammatories help your body recover from these exertions, as well as reducing pain and swelling. Fish and vegetables are great sources of anti-inflammatories, so including them in your post-workout meal is always a good idea.

In a more general sense, the other key elements for maximising the performance of your body are antioxidants. They help keep your physiological processes running smoothly, even at the level of your cells. For example, **antioxidants are crucial in limiting the attack on your cells from free radicals, which are molecules that break down the bonds between other, healthy, molecules in your cells**. Fruit, vegies and ingredients like flaxseed are highly effective antioxidants. Given that your cells are also involved in the synthesis of protein, you can see how what you eat is supremely important in terms of how your body performs, and that a lot of the nutritional benefit you derive from the food you take in gets combined with other nutrients for maximum effect. That's why a balanced diet, high in lean protein, vegetables, whole-foods and with a smattering of superfoods is the best way to ensure you remain fit and healthy.

# the *SUPER*foods

# Vegetables

## Asparagus

Full of folate . . .
and frickin' tasty

I get excited when asparagus starts to come into season. The time when it is at its best is quite short – from spring to summer – so I make sure I eat it whenever I can while it's at its finest . . . and cheapest.

Asparagus is an antioxidant, low in cholesterol and high in fibre. But the headline here is the amount of folate it contains. Folate is crucial to the maintenance and production of cells throughout the body, including the brain. **Boosting folate intake is thought to have a positive effect on those who suffer from mild depression.**

A happy-making food that tastes great? Sign me up!

## Beetroot

Pumping purply
goodness

There's just something about the colour of beetroot that gets me excited to eat it – how can you not love that purple? Fortunately, beetroot is not just pretty; it's good for you as well.

**The antioxidants and folate that beetroot contains are helpful in maintaining the function of the liver** – the organ that stores vitamins, sugar and iron to give your body energy and that clears your blood of toxins. It also contains betacyanin, which can be useful in protecting against cancer.

## Broccoli

These bushy, bobbled
flower heads are great
for detox

A lot of people tell me they don't like broccoli, but I reckon its a hangover from being forced to eat it, boiled to within an inch of disintegrating – believe me, you need to get this superfood back into your diet. **It's an anti-cancer, cell-building, vitamin-packing *beast* of a vegetable.**

Broccoli contains good levels of vitamins C, A and K, which are all essential for good health. It also offers many trace minerals that our bodies need, including potassium and magnesium.

The robustness of this vegie also means you can use it in a number of ways, from simple steaming that keeps its crunch to baking it in the oven.

It's true: brussels sprouts contain awesome amounts of protein for a vegetable. And **given that protein is the building block of muscle, eating your sprouts is great way to maximise the benefits of your exercise regime.** It also means that you can have them instead of meat when you are having a vegetarian day. With lots of vitamin C and all the anti-cancer benefits that come with being one of the cruciferous family, these little beauties shouldn't just be relegated to a once-in-a-blue-moon occasion. Look at what we're missing out on!

Brussels are actually a lot more versatile than many of us might think – they are great in stir-fries, for instance.

# Brussels sprouts

This much protein in a vegetable? WOW!

Cruciferous vegetables like cabbage – and including broccoli, brussels sprouts, cauliflower, cabbage and kale – are all-round good for you. All of them have been **linked with having a preventative effect in the human body against certain kinds of cancer**, including lung, breast and colon diseases. Research into their properties is ongoing, but it is thought that substances called glucosinolates are the active ingredients.

That's a pretty good reason to get this superfood into your diet right there. But the benefits don't stop there. Flavonoids are in there too, as is a heap of vitamins K and C. Did you know, by the way, that red cabbage has around six times as much vitamin C as the white version?

# Cabbage

Cruciferous, so anti-cancer

While leafy greens are superb providers of nutritional content, their white cousin, cauliflower, is no slouch either, and thoroughly deserves a place on my superfoods list. **Its antioxidant and anti-inflammatory properties help keep your cells and physiological functions in good shape**, which makes this vegetable a great complement to any training regime. If you are eating right, your body will perform better when you push it during training.

These effects are compounded in cauliflower by the vitamin B6 it contains, which helps brain function. With benefits like that, who wouldn't want some?

# Cauliflower

Lots of nutrients that give exercisers energy

the *super*foods   7

# Kale

Curly or straight,
kale totally rocks

Kale is another of those ingredients around which the term 'superfood' gets bandied about a lot. In this case, DO believe the hype!

As a leafy green vegetable, **kale contains a lot of carotenoids. These help protect your cells from free radicals, which are weak molecules that look to bond with, and break down, stronger ones.** Carotenoids are like nutritional bounty hunters, rounding up and neutralising these destructive interlopers. Loaded with vitamin C and vitamin A, kale is great for detoxing and also has anti-imflammatory benefits. Your body will thank you every time you eat it.

# Mushrooms

Antioxidant and
pro-immunity:
I'll vote for that

One of the key nutrients that mushrooms provide is selenium. An antioxidant compound, selenium helps support your cells and so can help prevent the development of chronic diseases. It also **boosts your immune system, and is therefore handy for maintaining good health.**

The other awesome thing about mushrooms is that they are so dense and satisfying that they make the perfect replacement for meat in many dishes. As they are **virtually fat-free**, making the switch means you are lowering the caloric value of your meal, without sacrificing any of the satisfaction or taste. With mushrooms on the plate, I never feel I'm missing something.

# Silverbeet

So many vitamins,
so few calories

As an ingredient, silverbeet can be a bit tricky. The stalks and leaves tend to need different cooking times, so have to be separated and added in two lots. However, it's worth it when you consider how many nutrients these leafy greens deliver – **silverbeet contains good levels of 16 vitamins and minerals!**

Chief among these is magnesium. This mineral is involved in hundreds of different metabolic processes in the body, including helping our brains to function properly. A lot of people don't get enough magnesium in their diet, so silverbeet, being so goddamn tasty, is the ideal way to make sure you get what you need.

# Spinach

Hands down,
King of the Vegies

So, just like Batman is at the top of the tree when it comes to superheroes – am I right? (we can argue about that one later!) – so spinach may just take the crown of head honcho when it comes to vegetables. It's simple – look at this list of nutrients it contains:

Folate
Magnesium
Calcium
Iron
Vitamin A
Vitamin C
Betacarotene
Potassium

Plus (I know! What more can there be?) it is **super-low in calories** – less than 25 in every 100 grams. When a vegetable is this good for you, it's a crime not to get it into your diet.

# Watercress

The peppery tang
delivers powerful
protection

Give me an A! Give me a C! Give me a D! Give me a K! Give me a B! What have you got? No, I know it doesn't spell anything, but you do have a list of all the vitamins that watercress contains.

Let's look at just one of them. **Vitamin K is essential for your blood.** It helps it to clot should you cut yourself, and it helps to prevent bruising. Having healthy blood flow also reduces the risk of heart disease and helps your body perform when you exercise.

Watercress also has **anti-cancer and antioxidant** properties. Seriously, I'm leading the cheer squad for this one.

# Fruit

## Apples

The ultimate
low-calorie snack

'An apple a day keeps the doctor away.' We've all heard that one, right? And you know what? It could just be right. **Apples certainly help to keep your cardiovascular and digestive systems in good nick.**

They are also compact, efficient nutrient- and flavour-delivery systems. What does that mean? They're great to throw in your bag as a snack when you're on the go! Apples also come in a wonderful range of varieties, each with a different flavour. Some are a little more tart, while others yield a soft sweetness. I've used Red Delicious in several recipes, and they are particularly powerful on the antioxidant front.

Don't peel your apples; the skin is where a lot of the nutrients hang out.

## Blueberries

Use the bloobs –
they are seriously
good for you

I sometimes wonder how something so small can pack so many good things in. Blueberries are simply wonderful. They are kind of facilitators – **they help all of the body's systems function correctly.** Flavonoids and antioxidants help keep your cells healthy (including those in your brain, which will slow cognitive decline), fibre aids digestion, while niacin is crucial to cardiovascular health.

Blueberries also have a vividly intense flavour. Just pop a raw one in your mouth and crack through the skin; the sheer fruitiness that bursts out is amazing. For me, this makes them a great snack food. You get a sweet treat from nature's lolly shop.

## Cranberries

Potent flavour
bursts that are
good for you too

These ruby berries may be small but they are pretty powerful on the nutritional front. **One of their most potent weapons is the ability to fight bacteria,** particularly in the digestive system. Their antioxidant capacity is allied to both anti-cancer and anti-inflammatory benefits. Cranberries also offer decent levels of an array of vitamins and a hit of fibre. Pretty impressive for such a little thing.

Drinking cranberry juice is good (just make sure that it has no added sugar), but you get more benefit if you eat the whole fruit. In Australia, this will typically be either frozen or dried cranberries. Both contain similar levels of vitamins and minerals (although beware of dried cranberries that have a lot of added sugar). I like to snack on them, but they are also awesome in salads.

## Goji berries

*Forget the myths –
just taste the goodness*

Goji berries are kind of a victim of their own success. For many people they seem like the epitome of hard-to-get, mystical ingredients that get tagged as 'superfoods'. But, you know what, they are actually awesome. And because they have become more popular as people have realised their nutritional potential, they are more easily available and more affordable than ever before.

So what is it that makes these little red berries worthy of a place on my list? Well, for a start they are high in calcium. **We don't often associate fruit with calcium, but these bad boys are loaded with it.** They also contain lots of different minerals, vitamins and carotenoids, including lutein, which is useful in warding off eye diseases.

## Kiwifruit

*Seriously,
how much
vitamin C?*

Yep, pound for pound (although I'm not suggesting you eat a pound in one sitting!), **kiwifruit pack in more vitamin C than oranges . . . and oranges are pretty damn dosed with it!** Vitamin C plays an important role in protecting our cells from attack by free radicals, so making sure you get enough helps fight disease all over the body.

Kiwifruit are also a good source of fibre, which is good for colon health. With that double dose of goodness, you'd be mad not to get them into your diet!

## Oranges

*Versatile and packed
with vitamins*

We all know that oranges contain heaps of vitamin C, and for that alone, they are worthy additions to your diet. But the fact that they also offer a range of other nutrients really takes them into superfood territory.

Did you know, for example, that **oranges contain several types of flavonoids that all have an antioxidant effect on the body?** Or that they are loaded with pectin, a type of fibre that helps keep your intestines healthy? Add a little grated zest to your cereal for extra zing and goodness.

Oranges are also versatile. You can keep them in your kitchen for a good few days before they start to go off, so they are handy for juicing, adding to your breakfast cereal or popping into a salad.

# Raspberries

Who needs candy
when you've got
sweet raspberries?

I could quite happily eat a handful of raspberries in place of a dessert and never feel like I'm missing out. As a snack, they work perfectly and, of course, they add a sparkle to any breakfast.

When it comes to nutritional content, they're not half bad, either. **As well as giving you good levels of vitamin C, raspberries offer two 'f's: flavonoids and folate.** The former is a cell protector, and is one of the compounds that give fruits and vegetables their colour. Folate helps your body when it is generating new cells, making sure they develop correctly. This is particularly prevalent in the brain, and eating foods rich in folate can help your brain cells stay healthy, warding off degenerative diseases such as Alzheimer's.

# Tomatoes

Cook 'em, munch 'em
raw, whatever – they
help prevent cancer

Research has suggested that **eating tomatoes can have a beneficial effect in preventing cancer, particularly prostate and breast**. So everyone should be getting some into their diet.

These incredible fruits don't just stop there – they are benevolent little blighters, giving you good levels of an array of nutrients. These include flavonoids and carotenoids that fight off chemical attacks on your cells. Magnesium's in there, helping your brain function correctly, while tomatoes are also a great antioxidant ingredient. Throw in a smattering of vitamins and you've got one hell of an awesome fruit.

# Nuts, Grains & Seeds

Zinc is an awesome mineral. It is involved in ensuring the proper function of hundreds of chemical and metabolic processes that go on in our bodies. These include the immune and reproductive systems. Zinc also helps the body synthesise protein, which is key to building strong muscles.

Almonds are naturally full of zinc. They also have **good levels of calcium, potassium and magnesium.** Magnesium helps the enzymes in our brains to function correctly.

For me, almonds make a great snack. Portion them out into separate zip-lock bags and they are all ready to go when you head out in the morning.

Chia seeds are derived from plants that are actually part of the mint family. The little brown seeds are usually little more than a millimetre in diameter, but they are **bursting at the seams with superfood goodness**.

Chief among their benefits is omega-3, good for the brain and the heart. They are also a good source of protein, and are gluten-free, making them ideal for those with an intolerance.

Combined with **a high proportion of calcium, fibre and antioxidants**, it's amazing what chia seeds contain. Good things come in small packages, obviously.

We often think that omega-3 acids only come from meat, fish and eggs – animal sources, basically. But flaxseed is another good source of this brain-boosting nutrient, and so is **a perfect superfood for vegetarians**.

The good stuff doesn't stop there either. Flaxseed is also a powerful antioxidant, is **loaded with fibre and contains high levels of vitamin E**. This particular vitamin helps protect your cells from attack by free radicals, particularly in the liver. It is also thought to aid the fight against cancer and cardiovascular disease.

Flaxseed is perfect for adding to your breakfast cereal or sprinkled on yoghurt with fruit. You can also add it to salads.

## Almonds

Lots of zinc to help
your body function
at its best

## Chia seeds

Tiny little bombs
of omega-3 power

## Flaxseed

Good for heart health –
so good for training

## Oats

A superb
provider
of fibre

There's a good reason why porridge has been a popular breakfast cereal for so long – oats fill you up. With tons of fibre, they help keep you sated until lunchtime, minimising the desire for a high-calorie mid-morning snack to keep you going. The fibre – the soluble and insoluble kind, both of which oats contain and which your body needs to function well – also **helps keep your digestive system in good nick**.

Oats are also beneficial in other respects. They help protect the health of your cardiovascular system, and provide trace elements such as zinc and magnesium, which **assist cell and metabolic functions**.

## Walnuts

A little goes a
long way with
these nutrient
powerhouses

These delicious, knobbly nuts are another **good source of powerful omega-3 fatty acids**. This brain-boosting element is accompanied in its mission in walnuts by good levels of protein and folate. **Walnuts can also help reduce your cholesterol.**

As with many nuts, I do have to sound a mini warning, though. Walnuts are relatively high in calories, so don't eat too many. However, all the recipes I'll give you that include these delicious nuts use small amounts, which means you get all the benefits without a caloric downside.

## Wheatgerm

Fibre, protein,
vitamins –
it's all good

Wheatgerm is actually the reproductive part of a wheat grain's kernel. The name has nothing to do with infection; rather, it comes from the word 'germination'. Even then, it is only a very small percentage of the kernel, but my, it is super-stuffed with good things.

Wheatgerm provides **an easy way to get protein into your diet** – so is great for vegetarians – and is also reasonably high in fibre. It also contains a number of B vitamins that are essential to good cardiovascular health.

Store in a sealed container for adding to everything from cereal and smoothies to salads and stews.

# Fish

## Salmon

Sustainable
salmon =
a sensational
superfood

Besides that lovely silken texture and rich flavour, I always feel that I can virtually *taste* the goodness in salmon. Perhaps it's that glisten it has, reminding me of all the omega-3 fatty acids it contains, which **boost brain function**. Maybe it's that deep orange colour that sparks thoughts of all the vitamin D the flesh contains, the same vitamin we get from sunshine.

I also like the fact that salmon is so easy to use. I find it works perfectly in salads for lunch and sandwiches for lunch boxes. However, like all fish purchases, try to **ensure your salmon comes from a sustainable fishery**, preferably wild rather than farmed.

## Sardines

Little silver flashes
of amazing protein

Sardines have, in recent years, been trumpeted as the salvation for fish-eaters. **Packed with omega-3 fatty acids that are beneficial to brain function, and with lots of protein without many calories**, they have also been a sustainable source of fish. However, along with many other species in the oceans, the sardine population is under more and more pressure as demand increases. Always check that the fish you buy has come from a sustainable source and regularly consult information from the Australian Marine Conservation Society about which seafood is under threat, as this changes quite often.

So, once you have your sustainable sardines, there are so many wonderful things you can do with them, from a sandwich to a salad to simple grilling – **try some on the barbecue this summer**.

# Beans

## Chickpeas

Multitudes
of minerals

These nutty-tasting beans are great additions to everything from salads and soups to stews. I always have a couple of cans in the pantry.

Besides being versatile, chickpeas deliver a variety of trace elements. **Iron, copper, zinc and magnesium are all present, serving to keep your body running at its best.** Folate helps your brain function, while fibre aids your digestive system. All in all, that's a pretty powerful cocktail of nutrients.

# Dairy

## Yoghurt

My dairy darling
when it comes
to calcium

It's becoming more and more common knowledge that the live cultures in yoghurt help keep our digestive systems functioning well. And, being made from milk, yoghurt also contains **a lot of calcium, which is good for everyone's skeleton, from bone development in infants, to maintaining bone density in the elderly**. But did you know that yoghurt is also good for your brain? It contains good levels of magnesium, which helps facilitate metabolic functions, particularly in the grey matter upstairs.

It can be easy to see yoghurt just as something to add to your breakfast cereal or as a quick snack – and, don't get me wrong, it is perfect for both those things – but it is a much more versatile ingredient than that. I use it in soups, as a dressing for salads and an accompaniment to stews – there are so many ways to love this ingredient.

# Eggs

Perfect packages
of protein

One of the great things about eggs is the sheer number of ways that your can cook them – poaching, baking, boiling and so on. However, I recommend that you keep fried eggs to a minimum so you don't overdo it on the cooking oil.

When you look at all the nutrients that eggs contain inside those fragile shells, it can blow your mind: **protein, omega-3 fats, zinc and several crucial vitamins**. They are also a good source of one of the amino acids the body uses to produce serotonin – the feel-good hormone. Go for organic, free-range varieties whenever possible, for healthier hens and healthier eggs.

# Meat

# Calves' liver

Protein and iron –
what a double
whammy!

Some people are put off liver, thinking that it has too strong a taste or simply not knowing how to cook it. Calves' liver is the perfect ingredient to introduce this meat – and all its benefits – into your diet. The flavour is subtle and it can be cooked in a matter of minutes.

Calves' liver is high in protein and iron, but also **contains lots of vitamin B12, which is used all around the body, helping you form red blood cells and protecting your neurological health.** The meat also contains selenium, which is an active ingredient in protecting your body from infection.

# Kangaroo

Truly Aussie,
truly healthy

I'm sure we could all make a list of what Australia is great for. High on mine would be producing this amazing meat. **Packed with protein and with less than two per cent fat, it is one of the leanest meats available.** As such, it is low calorie and quick to cook – a couple of minutes on the char-grill pan or the barbecue and you're good to go.

Kangaroo is also banging with zinc and iron. The former is important for cell maintenance, while the latter helps deliver oxygen to your cells, particularly the proteins in your muscles, making kangaroo an excellent dietary addition for when you're exercising.

oats

mushrooms

yoghurt

kiwifruit

goji berries

# *SUPER* BREAKFAST

eeds

eggs

tomatoes

wheatgerm

ange

spinach

walnuts

A smoothie is a great way to start the morning. In each of the three options I've given you here, there are a host of superfoods and lots of other good stuff to put a spring in your step for the day ahead.

# Smoothie trio

## Green smoothie

SERVES 2
PREP 5 minutes
CAL PER SERVE 180

2 ripe **kiwifruit**, peeled and
  chopped
½ cup baby **spinach** leaves
½ cup (125 ml) freshly squeezed
  **orange** juice
½ cup (125 ml) no-fat natural
  **yoghurt**

1. Combine all the ingredients in a blender and blend until smooth.

## Berry smoothie

SERVES 2
PREP 5 minutes
CAL PER SERVE 174

200 g silken firm tofu, drained
½ cup (125 ml) freshly squeezed
  **orange** juice
½ cup (125 ml) low-cal milk
½ cup frozen mixed **berries**,
  just thawed

1. Combine all the ingredients in a blender and blend until smooth.

## Tropical smoothie

SERVES 2
PREP 5 minutes
CAL PER SERVE 169

1 large mango, peeled and
  deseeded
½ cup (125 ml) no-fat natural
  **yoghurt**
½ cup (125 ml) low-cal milk
2 tablespoons chopped mint leaves
2 teaspoons grated fresh ginger
2 teaspoons raw **wheatgerm**
2 passionfruit, pulp removed

1. Combine the mango, yoghurt, milk, mint, ginger and wheatgerm in a blender and blend until smooth. Pour into two glasses and stir in the passionfruit pulp.

TIP
Always use ripe fruit to get the most sweetness.

All the fruit in this recipe makes for a sweetly nutritious breakfast. The nuts add a hit of antioxidants and protein – but don't overdo them, as they are quite high in fat.

# Fruit & nut wheat biscuits

SERVES 2
PREP 10 minutes
COOK 5 minutes
CAL PER SERVE 400

1½ tablespoons chopped
   macadamia nuts
1 tablespoon pistachio nuts
100 g red seedless grapes,
   halved
125 g rockmelon, peeled,
   deseeded and chopped
2 **kiwifruit**, peeled and diced
½ mango, peeled and diced
4 wheat biscuits
1 cup (250 ml) low-cal milk

**1.** Place the macadamia and pistachio nuts in a medium frying pan on medium–high. Cook, stirring, for 4 minutes or until toasted. Set aside.

**2.** Arrange the fruit and biscuits in two bowls. Sprinkle with the nuts and then add the milk to serve.

TIP
There's nothing like freshly toasted nuts but if you haven't got the time in the morning, make a batch every thee or four days and, once cooled, keep in an airtight container in a cool place.

VARIATION
Replace the wheat biscuits with 1¼ cups bran cereal (423 cal per serve).

Store-bought muesli can often contain lots of added sugar –
it's much better to make your own. The sweetness here comes
from the cranberries and mango, while the flaxseed and
wheatgerm really crank this up into 'super' territory.

# Super muesli

SERVES 2
PREP 5 minutes
CAL PER SERVE 392

⅔ cup (50 g) bran
½ cup (45 g) traditional rolled **oats**
¼ cup (35 g) dried **cranberries**
20 g dried mango, chopped
2 tablespoons raw **wheatgerm**
1 tablespoon **flaxseed**
½ mango, peeled and chopped
1 cup (250 ml) low-cal milk

**1.** Combine the bran, oats, cranberries, dried mango, wheatgerm
and flaxseed in a bowl. Divide between two serving bowls. Add fresh
mango and milk to serve.

TIP
You can make a big batch of this super muesli and store it in
an airtight container in a cool dry place for up to one month
(346 cal per 100 g/1 cup).

VARIATION
Replace the mango with ½ cup drained apricot halves in natural
juice and 50 g raspberries (400 cal per serve).

Simple, tasty, low-calorie and filling – I love this breakfast.
The chia seeds keep their crunch while the bran softens.
And those two ingredients give you a good dose of fibre
to start your day.

# Bran & citrus brekkie

SERVES 2
PREP 10 minutes
CAL PER SERVE 408

**2 oranges**
**1 white grapefruit**
**1 ruby grapefruit**
**1¼ cups (90 g) bran**
**1½ tablespoons white chia seeds**
**1 cup (250 ml) low-cal milk**

1. Segment the oranges and grapefruits. Cut off the ends of the fruit so they sit flat. Use a knife to slice off the skin, being careful not to cut into the flesh. Hold the fruit over a bowl to catch the juice. Cut down either side of the white membrane between the segments then push gently so the segments slip out. Squeeze the remaining fruit to extract the juice.

2. Divide the bran and chia seeds between two bowls. Add the citrus segments and top with the milk to serve.

TIP
Neat citrus segments give a professional look to any dish. It's the same technique for all citrus and once you've practised on a few fruit you'll quickly get the hang of it. And don't waste the juice. Enjoy it as a small vitamin shot or keep it for dressings, sauces or smoothies.

Muesli is an awesome way to get lots of nutrients in one hit. I'm always looking for new recipe ideas to vary this breakfast powerhouse, and adding quinoa makes a delicious change. Scale up the amounts and make a batch to keep in the fridge for up to three days for an easy start to the morning.

# Quinoa bircher muesli

1. Place the quinoa in a small saucepan with ½ cup (125 ml) water and bring to the boil. Reduce the heat to low and simmer, covered, for 15 minutes or until the water has been absorbed. Allow to cool slightly.

2. Place the quinoa in a medium bowl with the oats, milk, berries and almonds. Stir and place in the fridge, covered with plastic wrap, overnight.

3. Stir in the flaxseed and chia seeds and divide between two bowls. Top with the passionfruit and kiwifruit to serve.

TIP
Preparing this breakfast the night before means less stress in the morning but it also helps all the flavours to infuse and gives the dish a beautiful creaminess.

SERVES 2
PREP 10 minutes,
    plus overnight soaking
COOK 15 minutes
CAL PER SERVE 408

¼ cup (50 g) red quinoa,
    rinsed and drained
¼ cup traditional rolled oats
1 cup (250 ml) low-cal milk
2 tablespoons goji berries
2 tablespoons dried cranberries
2 tablespoons raw almonds,
    coarsely chopped
3 teaspoons flaxseed
3 teaspoons white chia seeds
1 passionfruit, halved
1 kiwifruit, peeled and diced

Quinoa just missed out on making my superfoods list, but it's a pretty generous food when it comes to nutrients. Antioxidants and vitamins, as well as protein, make it a big-hitter. I love the basil in this recipe – it may seem a little odd at first glance, but I assure you, it really works.

# Sweet quinoa tabouleh

SERVES 2
PREP 5 minutes
COOK 15 minutes
CAL PER SERVE 310

½ cup (140 g) white quinoa,
    rinsed and drained
250 g strawberries, hulled
    and chopped
2 **oranges**, segmented,
    juice reserved
2 tablespoons small basil leaves
½ cup (190 g) no-fat natural
    **yoghurt**
1½ tablespoons honey

1. Place the quinoa in a small saucepan with 1 cup (250 ml) water. Bring to the boil. Cover and reduce the heat to low. Cook for 15 minutes or until the water has been absorbed and the quinoa is tender.

2. Toss the strawberries, orange segments and reserved orange juice through the warm quinoa. Divide between two bowls and sprinkle with the basil. Serve with the yoghurt and honey.

TIP
Segment the oranges over a bowl to catch the juices (see page 26).

VARIATION
Replace the oranges with a sliced mango and the strawberries and basil with 200 g blueberries (417 cal per serve).

The chia seeds and walnuts give a great crunch to this warm and comforting porridge. Add a little boiling water to adjust the consistency and sprinkle with a little extra cinnamon before reaching for the sugar or honey.

# Oat porridge with apple & walnuts

SERVES 2
PREP 10 minutes
COOK 5 minutes
CAL PER SERVE 402

¾ cup traditional rolled **oats**
2 Red Delicious **apples**,
    coarsely grated
1½ tablespoons raw **wheatgerm**
1 tablespoon white **chia seeds**
¼ teaspoon ground cinnamon,
    plus extra to sprinkle
¼ cup chopped **walnuts**, toasted

1.  Place the oats and 1¾ cups (430 ml) water in a small saucepan over medium heat. Bring to the boil. Reduce the heat to low and cook for 5 minutes, stirring occasionally. Stir in the apple, wheatgerm, chia seeds and cinnamon.

2.  Divide the oats between two bowls and sprinkle with the walnuts and extra cinnamon to serve.

TIP
To cook the oats in the microwave, place the oats and the water in a microwave-proof bowl and microwave on high (100 per cent) for 4½ minutes.

VARIATION
Try an Indian variation with 1½ cups diced fresh mango, ¼ cup pistachios and ground cardamom to taste (363 cal per serve).

For me, one of the glories of this dish is the combination of textures. A crunchy crumpet with smooth ricotta and fresh fruit is just so exciting. If you've ever skipped breakfast because you thought it was too boring, a) don't skip breakfast (it usually means you end up snacking mid-morning on high-calorie crap when your energy levels drop) and b) try this!

# Fruit & ricotta crumpets

1. Combine the ricotta, orange zest and juice in a small bowl.

2. Spread the crumpets with the ricotta mixture and top with the fruit.

TIP
You can prepare the orange ricotta mixture the night before and store it in the fridge.

VARIATIONS
Transform this breakfast into a dessert by drizzling each serve with 1 teaspoon honey (332 cal per serve).

You can also top these sweet breakfasts with 200 g sliced strawberries and 1 tablespoon shredded basil (277 cal per serve).

SERVES 2
PREP 10 minutes
CAL PER SERVE 310

½ cup (120 g) fresh low-cal
   ricotta cheese
½ teaspoon finely grated
   **orange** zest
2 tablespoons **orange** juice
2 wholemeal crumpets, toasted
2 **kiwifruit**, peeled, halved
   and sliced
50 g **blueberries**

The 'meaty' texture of mushrooms means this breakfast feels filling without loading you up with calories. Even the parsley in this recipe is good for you, with lots of iron and vitamin C, while the sumac adds a tasty tang.

# Spicy mushrooms on cheesy toast

SERVES 2
PREP 10 minutes
COOK 10 minutes
CAL PER SERVE 386

3 teaspoons olive oil
300 g mixed **mushrooms**, chopped
2 garlic cloves, crushed
2 tablespoons coarsely chopped
   fresh flat-leaf parsley,
   plus extra to serve
freshly ground black pepper
½ teaspoon sumac
1 bunch English **spinach**,
   trimmed and washed
⅓ cup (65 g) low-cal cottage cheese
4 slices wholegrain & oats bread
   (180 g), toasted

1. Heat the olive oil in a large frying pan on high. Cook the mushrooms, stirring, for 5 minutes or until browned. Stir in the garlic and parsley. Cook for 1 minute or until fragrant. Season with black pepper and sprinkle with the sumac.

2. Meanwhile, place the spinach in a microwave-safe bowl. Microwave, covered, for 1 minute or until wilted. Drain.

3. Spread the cottage cheese over the toast. Top with the mushrooms. Sprinkle the extra parsley over the top and serve with the spinach alongside.

TIP
I use a mix of button, brown, shiitake and enoki mushrooms. Quarter the larger mushrooms and add the enoki toward the end as they cook much more quickly.

VARIATION
You can add a poached egg when you have more time (459 cal per serve).

A hearty breakfast for a crisp autumn day. The fibre in the chickpeas keeps you full until lunchtime, so you won't feel the need for a pick-me-up snack. And cooking tomatoes actually *increases* the nutritional content from their raw state. This dish also makes for a wicked weekend lunch.

# Moroccan eggs

1. Heat the oil in a large frying pan on medium–high. Cook the capsicum, stirring, for 3 minutes. Add the onion and cook, stirring, for another 7 minutes or until the onion is softened and browned. Add the spices and garlic and cook, stirring, for 1 minute or until fragrant. Stir in the chickpeas, tomatoes and ¼ cup (60 ml) water. Simmer, covered, for 5 minutes for the flavours to infuse.

2. Make four holes in the capsicum mixture and crack an egg into each hole. Cook, covered but with the lid askew, for 7–8 minutes for the egg whites to set or until cooked to your liking. Season with black pepper.

3. Sprinkle with the coriander sprigs and serve with the toast alongside.

TIPS
You can also freeze the capsicum mixture after step 1 in individual containers.

If you prefer, you can make this recipe in individual serving dishes.

SERVES 4
PREP 10 minutes
COOK 25 minutes
CAL PER SERVE 373

2 teaspoons olive oil
3 yellow capsicums, thinly sliced
1 large onion, thinly sliced
1½ teaspoons ground cumin
1 teaspoon ground coriander
2 garlic cloves, crushed
2 x 400 g cans **chickpeas**, drained and rinsed
400 g can diced **tomatoes**
4 **eggs**
freshly ground black pepper
coriander sprigs, to serve
4 slices wholemeal sourdough (140 g), toasted

This is simply a sublime combination of flavours. And, not only does it contain three superfoods, you've also got some avocado in there, which is full of the 'good' mono-unsaturated fats that help keep your heart healthy and give you energy for exercise.

# Avocado, salmon & poached egg

SERVES 2
PREP 5 minutes
COOK 10 minutes
CAL PER SERVE 363

1 teaspoon white vinegar
2 **eggs**
1 wholemeal English muffin (75 g),
    split and toasted
15 g **watercress** sprigs
½ avocado, sliced
150 g smoked **salmon**, torn
    into bite-sized pieces
1 tablespoon chopped
    fresh chives
**freshly ground black pepper**

1.  Half-fill a medium saucepan with water and add the vinegar. Place over medium–high heat and bring almost to the boil. Reduce the heat slightly and stir the water to create a whirlpool. Carefully crack one egg on the side of the saucepan and release the contents into the middle of the whirlpool. Fish the poached egg out with a slotted spoon after 2 minutes for a softie, or after 3 minutes for a hardie. Repeat with the second egg.

2.  Meanwhile, top the muffins with the watercress, avocado and smoked salmon. Top with the eggs. Sprinkle the chives over and season with black pepper.

TIP
Watercress doesn't last long in the fridge. Use it up quickly in salads, sandwiches, spring rolls or as a fresh side for grilled meat. If it's looking sad, leave it to stand in a bowl of cold water in the fridge for a few hours until it perks up.

I love constructing these little beauties then savouring the aromas as they bake in the oven. They tend to work for me as a weekend brekkie, but this recipe also makes an ideal spring brunch with friends.

# Oeuf cocotte

SERVES 2
PREP 10 minutes
COOK 15 minutes
CAL PER SERVE 350

olive oil spray
1 bunch **asparagus**, trimmed
   and cut into 2 cm pieces
½ **spring onion**, trimmed
   and thinly sliced
20 g **low-cal cheddar cheese**,
   grated
1 tablespoon **pistachio dukkah**
2 **eggs**
2 tablespoons **light thickened**
   **cream**
3 slices **wholegrain bread (120 g)**,
   toasted and cut in half
   on the diagonal

**1.** Preheat the oven to 180°C (160°C fan-forced). Lightly spray two ¾-cup (185 ml) capacity ramekins with oil.

**2.** Cook the asparagus in a small saucepan of boiling water for 2 minutes or until just tender. Drain and pat dry with kitchen paper.

**3.** Set aside the tips of the asparagus spears. Divide the remaining asparagus between the ramekins. Sprinkle with the spring onion, cheese and half of the dukkah. Carefully crack an egg into a small dish, then tip into a ramekin. Repeat with the remaining egg. Drizzle with the cream, being careful not to drizzle over the yolk. Sprinkle with the remaining dukkah.

**4.** Place the ramekins in a small roasting pan. Pour enough boiling water into the pan to come halfway up the sides of the ramekins. Bake in the oven for 10–12 minutes or until the white is set and the yolk is still runny, or until cooked to your liking.

**5.** Remove the ramekins from the oven and serve immediately, topped with the reserved asparagus tips and with the toast alongside.

Sometimes only a hot breakfast will do. Grilling your sausages and vegetables is a healthier way to cook them than frying. You also get that lovely extra tang from the slight charring, which combines well with the aromatic thyme.

# Breakfast grill

1. Lightly spray the vegetables with oil and sprinkle with thyme.

2. Heat a char-grill pan on medium–high. Cook the mushrooms for 12 minutes or until tender. After 4 minutes, add the sausages and cook, turning, for 8 minutes or until lightly charred and cooked through. After 6 minutes, add the tomatoes and asparagus and cook for 6 minutes or until tender.

3. Season with black pepper and serve sprinkled with the extra thyme leaves.

VARIATION
Instead of the chicken sausages, you could serve two lean grass-fed beef sausages (329 cal per serve) or scrambled eggs made with four eggs and ⅓ cup low-cal cottage cheese along with two slices of toasted wholemeal bread (303 cal per serve).

SERVES 2
PREP 5 minutes
COOK 15 minutes
CAL PER SERVE 333

olive oil spray
2 large field **mushrooms**
4 Roma **tomatoes**, halved
1 bunch **asparagus**, trimmed
3 teaspoons fresh thyme leaves,
    plus extra to serve
2 x 90 g lean chicken sausages
**freshly ground black pepper**

Who doesn't love a toasted sandwich? This version adds lots of superfood goodness and keeps the calorie count down. The chilli sauce gives it a lovely little kick.

# Turkey & cheese toastie

SERVES 2
PREP 5 minutes
COOK 5 minutes
CAL PER SERVE 385

**170 g Turkish bread**
**2 teaspoons chilli sauce**
**1 small tomato, sliced**
**40 g button mushrooms,**
  **thinly sliced**
**15 g baby spinach leaves,**
  **plus extra to serve**
**90 g cooked turkey, sliced**
**40 g low-cal cheddar cheese,**
  **thinly sliced**

1. Preheat a sandwich maker.

2. Cut the bread into two portions then split each portion in half. Spread the bases with the chilli sauce. Top with the tomato, mushroom, spinach, turkey and cheese. Finish with the remaining bread halves. Place in the sandwich maker and lower the lid. Toast for 3 minutes or until the cheese has melted and the bread is crisp. Cut into fingers and serve with the extra baby spinach alongside.

TIP
You can also make this toastie in a frying pan on medium–high heat. Place a heatproof plate on the bread to weigh it down and turn halfway through cooking to toast both sides.

**SUPER LUNCH**

eggs
mushrooms
spinach
asparagus
sardines
eeds
wheatgerm
yog
beetroot
mon
cabbag
tomatoes

One of my favourite lunch box recipes. With all the vitamins and nutrients in spinach and the omega-3 oils in salmon, these beauties will give you a body and brain boost to see you through till dinnertime.

# Salmon & cucumber rice paper rolls

SERVES 2
PREP 20 minutes
COOK 5 minutes
CAL PER SERVE 315

1 Lebanese cucumber, cut
   into batons
1 tablespoon rice-wine vinegar
¼ x 250 g packet rice vermicelli
   noodles
½ cup bean sprouts, tails removed
40 g baby **spinach** leaves, shredded
⅓ cup fresh mint, coarsely chopped,
   plus 6 extra leaves
6 round rice paper sheets
   (22 cm in diameter)
150 g smoked **salmon**

1. Combine the cucumber and vinegar in a bowl and set aside to pickle for 10 minutes. Drain.

2. Meanwhile, cook the noodles in boiling water for 2 minutes or until tender. Drain well then cool under cold running water and drain again. Combine in a bowl with the cucumber, bean sprouts, spinach and chopped mint.

3. One at a time, soak the rice paper sheets in room-temperature water for 30 seconds or until soft. Lift out and place on a clean tea towel to absorb any excess moisture. For each rice paper sheet, place one mint leaf on the upper half. Lay one-sixth of the smoked salmon over the mint leaf. Place one-sixth of the cucumber mixture on the lower half. Fold up the paper at the bottom, then fold the left and right sides over the filling. Roll up tightly to seal. Cover with a damp tea towel to prevent the roll from drying out. Repeat with the remaining rice paper and filling to make six rolls.

TIP
If you like to dip the rolls into sweet chilli sauce, remember that 1 tablespoon is 47 cal. One tablespoon of Vietnamese dipping sauce is 34 cal.

Everything about this sandwich just screams 'Eat me!' Horseradish cream and salmon is a classic combination, and I've widened the flavour spectrum by adding tangy beetroot and onion, cooling cucumber and earthy spinach. With all that, and three superfoods, a happy lunchtime is guaranteed!

# Beetroot & smoked salmon sandwich

SERVES 2
PREP 10 minutes
CAL PER SERVE 342

**4 slices wholegrain bread (160 g)**
**1½ tablespoons horseradish cream**
**2 teaspoons chopped fresh dill**
**½ Lebanese cucumber, thinly sliced**
**100 g smoked salmon**
**100 g sliced canned beetroot,**
  **drained**
**¼ small red onion, thinly sliced**
**20 g baby spinach leaves**

1. Spread the bread with the horseradish cream and sprinkle with the dill. Top two slices of bread with the cucumber, smoked salmon, beetroot, onion and baby spinach. Cover with the remaining bread slices, horseradish-side down.

TIP
Drain the beetroot on paper towel.

VARIATION
Try this sandwich with thinly sliced celery instead of cucumber to add some crunch (343 cal per serve).

Herring belong to the same family as sardines, and share many of the nutritional benefits. A great source of protein and omega-3s, herring are also low in cholesterol. With many trace elements and good levels of vitamins D and B12, herring should be on everyone's menu. As with their sardine cousins, make sure your fish are from a sustainable source.

# Herring on rye

1. Combine the fennel, cabbage, capers, shallot, oil and lemon juice in a bowl.

2. Top the toasted rye with the herring and the fennel mixture.

TIP
If packing a lunch box, pack the bread separately and toast at work.

VARIATIONS
You could also add half a thinly sliced Red Delicious apple (319 cal per serve).
Try this open sandwich with smoked salmon instead of herring (288 cal per serve).

SERVES 2
PREP 15 minutes
CAL PER SERVE 303

½ small fennel bulb, trimmed
    and shaved
50 g red **cabbage**, shaved
2 teaspoons baby capers
1 shallot, thinly sliced
1 teaspoon extra-virgin olive oil
1 teaspoon lemon juice
2 slices light rye bread (85 g),
    toasted
200 g marinated herring, drained

When I see the gloriously iridescent sardines poking out between the red of the tomato and the green of the salad leaves, I know that I'm definitely in for a tastebud-pleasing lunch. The pine nuts are a lovely addition. They are quite high in fat, so don't be tempted to add more to the recipe, but even this small amount gives you good levels of vitamin K and magnesium.

# Italian toasted sardine sandwich

MAKES 2
PREP 15 minutes
CAL PER SERVE 363

1 tablespoon pine nuts, toasted
¼ cup fresh flat-leaf parsley,
   finely chopped
1 garlic clove, crushed
1 tablespoon lemon juice
4 slices wholemeal sourdough
   (160 g), toasted
¼ small red onion, thinly sliced
1 Roma **tomato**, sliced
105 g can **sardines** in oil, drained
20 g mixed salad leaves

1. Crush the pine nuts in a mortar and pestle until coarsely ground. Add the parsley, garlic and lemon juice and crush until a coarse paste forms.

2. Spread the bread with the pine nut mixture. Top two slices of bread with the onion, tomato, sardines and mixed leaves. Cover with the remaining bread, spread-side down.

TIPS
You can use baby spinach instead of mixed leaves or make the spread with toasted almonds instead of pine nuts (349 cal per serve).

If taking to work for lunch, assemble the sandwich when ready to eat.

Something a bit out of the ordinary for your lunch box. You'll need
to prep it the day before, but the eggplant keeps in the fridge so you
can make extra for a couple of days' worth. It also provides you with
fibre and antioxidants.

# Spicy eggplant sandwich

1. Preheat the oven to 220°C (200°C fan-forced).

2. Place the eggplant on a baking tray and lightly spray with oil. Bake for
45 minutes or until tender. Set aside to cool slightly. Scoop out the flesh
with a spoon and discard the skin. Finely chop the flesh and place in a bowl
with the anchovy, garlic, cayenne pepper and paprika. Stir vigorously until
a coarse paste forms.

3. Spread the bread with the eggplant mixture. Top two slices with the
tomato, spinach, cheese, radish and cucumber. Cover with the remaining
bread, spread-side down.

TIPS

Make a double batch of eggplant and store in an airtight
container in the fridge for up to three days (87 cal per serve).
It works well in a chicken or roast beef sandwich with rocket
or you can enjoy it as a snack with vegetable sticks.

Roma tomatoes are the best for sandwiches as they are tasty
without being too juicy, so your bread won't go all soggy.

MAKES 2
PREP 20 minutes
COOK 45 minutes
CAL PER SERVE 330

300 g eggplant, halved
olive oil spray
3 anchovies, finely chopped
1 garlic clove, crushed
pinch cayenne pepper
pinch smoked sweet paprika
4 slices wholegrain bread (170 g)
1 Roma **tomato**, sliced
20 g baby **spinach** leaves
2 x 22 g slices low-cal cheddar
  cheese
1 radish, trimmed and thinly sliced
½ Lebanese cucumber, cut into
  ribbons

Horseradish cream is traditionally served with beef, but I reckon it gives a lovely piquant edge to chicken. The peppery watercress – with its oodles of vitamins – rounds this lunch box treat out nicely.

# Chicken & horseradish roll

**1.** Lightly spray a char-grill pan with oil and heat on medium–high. Cook the chicken for 3–4 minutes each side or until lightly charred and cooked through. Thinly slice on the diagonal.

**2.** Cut the baguette into two portions and split each portion in half lengthways, without cutting all the way through. Spread the inside with the horseradish cream then fill with the celery, watercress and warm chicken.

TIP
If packing for lunch, wait until the chicken is cool to fill the bread.

VARIATION
These flavours also go well with rare roast beef instead of the chicken (381 cal per serve).

MAKES 2
PREP 10 minutes
COOK 10 minutes
CAL PER SERVE 355

olive oil spray
150 g skinless chicken breast
35 cm wholemeal baguette (150 g)
1½ tablespoons horseradish cream
50 g celery, trimmed and thinly sliced on the diagonal
30 g watercress sprigs

Sweet beetroot combines with salty-tasting fetta cheese to delicious effect in this recipe. It works well both hot and cold. A great quick lunch to serve when guests unexpectedly pop by.

# Beetroot, fetta & dill frittata

SERVES 2
PREP 10 minutes
COOK 20 minutes
CAL PER SERVE 348

**2 teaspoons olive oil**
**440 g can whole baby beetroot,**
    **drained and halved if large**
**4 eggs**
**½ cup (60 g) frozen peas**
**3 spring onions, finely chopped**
**1 tablespoon chopped fresh dill**
**50 g low-cal fetta cheese, crumbled**
**freshly ground black pepper**
**mixed salad leaves, to serve**

1. Heat the oil in a small non-stick frying pan on high. Cook the beetroot, turning occasionally, for 10 minutes.

2. Meanwhile, lightly whisk the eggs with 1 tablespoon water in a medium bowl. Stir in the peas, spring onion and dill. Add the egg mixture to the pan. Sprinkle the fetta over and season with black pepper. Cook for 6–7 minutes, pulling in the sides with a spatula to help the runny egg cook faster. When most of the egg is set, place under a preheated medium grill for 3–4 minutes or until golden, puffed and set.

3. Serve with the mixed leaves alongside.

TIP
If packing this frittata for lunch, wait until it's cool before placing in an airtight container.

A frittata is a great dish to have in your repertoire. You can add pretty much anything you have to hand to it and it will provide a satisfying meal. Everyone has their favourite flavour combinations, but I like to get some superfoods in there. Besides the eggs that make up the base, broccoli, kale and tomatoes add colour, flavour and lots of vitamins and minerals.

# Kale frittata

SERVES 2
PREP 10 minutes
COOK 15 minutes
CAL PER SERVE 307

150 g **broccoli, cut into florets**
5 **eggs**
2 **tablespoons grated parmesan cheese**
**freshly ground black pepper**
2 **teaspoons olive oil**
100 g **kale, trimmed and leaves finely shredded**
100 g **cherry tomatoes, halved**

1. Steam the broccoli over a saucepan of boiling water for 2 minutes or until just tender.

2. Meanwhile, lightly whisk the eggs and parmesan together in a medium bowl. Season with black pepper.

3. Heat the oil in a small non-stick frying pan on high. Cook the kale, stirring, for 2–3 minutes or until wilted and bright green. Add the egg mixture to the pan. Top with the broccoli and tomatoes. Cook for 6–7 minutes, pulling in the sides with a spatula to help the runny egg cook faster. When most of the egg is set, place under a preheated grill for 2–3 minutes or until golden, puffed and set.

TIP
If packing this frittata for lunch, wait until it's cool to place it in an airtight container. You could use silverbeet or spinach leaves instead of kale.

Cabbage, apple and almonds – this recipe gives you three very different superfoods. But it also gives you so much more. Tuna and fennel are both packed with nutrients as well. The fish has lots of omega-3s and antioxidants like selenium, while fennel helps the functioning of your cardiovascular system.

# Tuna & fennel salad

1. Season the tuna with black pepper and the fennel seeds. Lightly spray a frying pan with oil and heat on high. Cook the tuna for 1–2 minutes each side for medium–rare or until cooked to your liking. Thickly slice.

2. Meanwhile, combine the oil and lemon juice in a small bowl and season with black pepper.

3. Place the fennel, cabbage and apple in a large bowl. Drizzle the dressing over and gently toss to coat. Arrange on serving plates, top with the tuna and sprinkle with the almonds.

TIP
A mandoline is the perfect tool to thinly shave the fennel and shred the cabbage. It's done in no time.

SERVES 2
PREP 15 minutes
COOK 5 minutes
CAL PER SERVE 382

**200 g piece tuna**
**freshly ground black pepper**
**½ teaspoon fennel seeds,**
  **coarsely crushed**
**olive oil spray**
**2 teaspoons extra-virgin olive oil**
**2 teaspoons lemon juice**
**½ large fennel bulb, shaved**
**100 g red cabbage, finely shredded**
**1 Red Delicious apple, cut into**
  **matchsticks**
**2 tablespoons chopped raw**
  **almonds**

Citrus fruit goes really well with shellfish. The grapefruit here adds a different flavour from the more traditional lemon or lime. I think it works sublimely. Look for fresh scallops that are hand-dived rather than dredged – a fishing technique that damages the seabed and destroys ocean life.

# Scallop & grapefruit salad

SERVES 2
PREP 15 minutes
COOK 5 minutes
CAL PER SERVE 356

**400 g fresh scallops, without roe**
**freshly ground black pepper**
**olive oil spray**
**1 tablespoon extra-virgin olive oil**
**3 teaspoons white balsamic**
  **dressing**
**80 g watercress sprigs**
**1 ruby grapefruit, segmented**
**1 celery stalk, trimmed and**
  **thinly sliced**

1. Season the scallops with black pepper. Lightly spray a char-grill pan with oil and heat on medium–high. Cook the scallops for 2 minutes each side or until lightly charred.

2. Combine the oil and balsamic dressing in a small bowl.

3. Arrange the watercress, grapefruit and celery on a serving plate. Top with the warm scallops. Drizzle with the dressing to serve.

TIP
Look out for fresh scallops as frozen scallops are engorged with water.

A true winter warmer. The cauliflower gives a lot of body – and, of course, nutrients – to the soup, while the tastes of the curry powder and parsnip mingle together and the wheatgerm provides an extra texture. You can toast the naan bread or heat it at a low temperature in the oven.

# Cauliflower & parsnip curry soup

SERVES 4
PREP 10 minutes
COOK 25 minutes
CAL PER SERVE 334

1 tablespoon olive oil
1 brown onion, chopped
1 tablespoon mild curry powder
1 kg **cauliflower**, trimmed
 and chopped
2 parsnips, peeled and chopped
2 cups (500 ml) low-sodium
 vegetable stock
¼ cup (25 g) raw **wheatgerm**
freshly ground black pepper
2 tablespoons chopped fresh chives
4 naan bread (185 g)

1. Heat the oil in a large saucepan over medium heat. Cook the onion, stirring, for 5 minutes or until softened. Stir in the curry powder and cook for 1 minute or until fragrant. Add the cauliflower, parsnip, stock, wheatgerm and 2 cups (500 ml) water and bring to the boil. Reduce the heat and simmer, covered, for 15 minutes or until tender. Transfer 2 cups of chopped vegetables to a bowl. Purée or blend the remaining soup until smooth. Return the chopped vegetables to the pan and season with black pepper.

2. Sprinkle with the chives and serve with warm naan bread alongside.

TIPS
Serve this soup drizzled with 2 tablespoons no-fat Greek-style yoghurt before sprinkling the chives (368 cal per serve).

You can freeze this soup in airtight containers for up to one month.

Soups are a great snack to have on hand in the freezer (174 cal without the bread).

A seriously seductive soup. Lustrous purple set off by white yoghurt and green dill – my mouth's watering just thinking about it! Even the dill gives you a lot of nutritional benefit, including calcium and flavonoids. Combined with the nourishing powerhouse that is beetroot, and the stratospheric vitamin C levels of red cabbage, this soup really packs a punch.

# Borscht

1. Heat the oil in a large saucepan over medium heat. Cook the beetroot, potatoes, onion, carrot, garlic, caraway seeds and bay leaf, stirring, for 10 minutes or until the vegetables start to soften. Add the stock and 2 cups (500 ml) water and bring to the boil. Reduce the heat to low and simmer, covered, for 30 minutes. Stir in the cabbage and simmer, covered, for 10 minutes or until the cabbage is just tender. Season with black pepper. Allow to cool slightly then blend the soup until smooth.

2. Divide the soup between four serving bowls. Add a dollop of yoghurt and sprinkle with the dill to serve.

TIPS

This soup will freeze in airtight containers for up to one month.

You can use a hand-held blender (and save on dishes) or a work-top blender to blend the soup. If using a work-top blender, don't forget to leave the vent open or the steam will build up in the blender and the lid will pop open.

SERVES 4
PREP 15 minutes
COOK 50 minutes
CAL PER SERVE 343

1 tablespoon olive oil
1 kg **beetroot**, trimmed, peeled and coarsely grated
400 g potatoes, peeled and diced
2 brown onions, finely chopped
2 carrots, diced
4 garlic cloves, thinly sliced
2 teaspoons caraway seeds
1 dried bay leaf
2 cups (500 ml) vegetable stock
200 g red **cabbage**, finely shredded
freshly ground black pepper
⅔ cup (190 g) no-fat Greek-style yoghurt
2 tablespoons finely chopped fresh dill

A good one to make when tomatoes are in season – and so at their tastiest and cheapest. This makes an ideal freezer meal. Just cook up a batch and store in individual portions. The wonderfully pungent basil contrasts divinely with the earthier tones of the vegetables and beans.

# Tomato & bean soup with basil

SERVES 4
PREP 15 minutes
COOK 50 minutes
CAL PER SERVE 335

**5 garlic cloves**
**1 tablespoon olive oil**
**1 brown onion, chopped**
**1 kg ripe tomatoes, chopped**
**2 x 400 g cans cannellini beans, drained and rinsed**
**2 cups (500 ml) low-sodium vegetable stock**
**½ cup finely shredded fresh basil leaves, plus extra leaves to serve**
**4 slices wholemeal sourdough (140 g)**

1. Coarsely chop four of the garlic cloves.

2. Heat the oil in a large saucepan over medium heat. Cook the onion and chopped garlic, stirring, for 5 minutes or until softened. Add the tomatoes and cook, stirring, for 10 minutes or until starting to break down. Add the beans, stock and 1 cup (250 ml) water. Bring to the boil. Reduce the heat and simmer, covered, for 25 minutes. Allow to cool slightly. Blend until smooth. Strain through a fine-meshed sieve into a clean saucepan. Reheat and stir in the shredded basil.

3. Meanwhile, toast the bread. Rub the remaining garlic clove onto the toast. Sprinkle the soup with the extra basil and serve with the garlic toast alongside.

TIPS
If using a work-top blender, make sure to leave the vent open or the steam will build up in the blender and the lid will pop open.

Use canned chopped tomatoes if making this soup in winter.

You can freeze this soup in airtight containers for up to one month.

VARIATION
You could stir 200 g finely shredded silverbeet or kale leaves through the piping hot soup (346 cal per serve). Only 242 cal per serve without the garlic bread.

A warm, creamy and comforting soup for when the nights are starting to draw in. Baking the onion means using less oil than frying, while the jasmine rice is wonderfully fragrant. In addition, mint is a good aid to digestion.

# Lebanese yoghurt & chickpea soup

1. Preheat the oven to 220°C (200°C fan-forced). Arrange half the onion on a tray lined with foil. Lightly spray with oil and season with black pepper. Toss to coat and bake for 20 minutes, tossing twice during the cooking time.

2. Meanwhile, heat the oil in a large saucepan over medium heat. Cook the garlic and remaining onion, stirring, for 10 minutes or until softened and golden. Add the chickpeas, rice and 2 cups (500 ml) water. Bring to the boil. Reduce the heat and simmer, covered, for 20 minutes or until the rice is tender. Stir in the yoghurt until combined and cook, covered, over low heat for 5 minutes.

3. Divide the soup between two bowls and sprinkle with the caramelised onion and mint to serve.

SERVES 2
PREP 10 minutes
COOK 35 minutes
CAL PER SERVE 405

2 brown onions, thinly sliced
olive oil spray
freshly ground black pepper
2 teaspoons olive oil
3 garlic cloves, crushed
400 g can **chickpeas**, drained
   and rinsed
⅓ cup (65 g) jasmine rice
⅔ cup (190 g) no-fat Greek-style
   yoghurt
2 tablespoons finely shredded
   fresh mint leaves

This soup takes a little time to make, but boy, is it worth it. Prawns contain a lot of protein, which is good for your muscles, and the chickpeas are pumping with fibre, which gives you energy.

# Prawn, chickpea & fennel soup

SERVES 2
PREP 20 minutes
COOK 55 minutes
CAL PER SERVE 363

500 g medium green prawns,
    peeled and deveined,
    heads reserved
2 teaspoons olive oil
freshly ground black pepper
1 large fennel bulb, thinly sliced
2 garlic cloves, thinly sliced
400 g can **chickpeas**, drained
    and rinsed
400 g can diced **tomatoes**
½ bunch **kale**, trimmed and
    finely shredded

1.  Place the prawn heads in a small saucepan and cover with cold water. Bring to the boil on medium heat and simmer for 20 minutes. Strain and return the liquid to the pan (discard the heads). Simmer for 5–10 minutes or until reduced to ½ cup (125 ml). Set aside.

2.  Heat half the oil in a large saucepan on high. Season the prawns with black pepper and cook for 2–3 minutes or until browned and opaque. Set aside.

3.  Heat the remaining oil in the same pan on medium. Cook the fennel and garlic, stirring, for 5 minutes or until starting to soften. Cook, covered, for another 5 minutes or until softened. Add the chickpeas, tomatoes, prawn stock and 1 cup (250 ml) water. Bring to the boil. Reduce the heat and simmer, covered, for 10 minutes for the flavours to infuse. Return the prawns to the pan, add the kale and cook, stirring, for 1 minute or until the kale wilts. Season with black pepper.

TIP
The prawn stock gives this soup an amazing flavour but if you haven't got the time, use 1½ cups (325 ml) fish stock instead of the prawn stock and water in step 3.

Chicken is a great source of protein. But it is also a good provider of B vitamins, folate and selenium. Organic, free-range birds are the way to go whenever possible. They are more ethical, less likely to contain added chemicals and, well, are just tastier.

# Chicken, corn, rice & silverbeet soup

SERVES 2
PREP 15 minutes
COOK 30 minutes
CAL PER SERVE 362

**200 g chicken breast, trimmed**
**⅓ cup (65 g) jasmine rice**
**1 corncob**
**50 g mushrooms, thinly sliced**
**8 silverbeet leaves, trimmed**
    **and finely shredded**
**2 spring onions, thinly sliced**

1.  Place the chicken in a medium saucepan with 4 cups (1 L) water. Bring to the boil over medium heat. Reduce the heat to low and barely simmer for 8 minutes. Remove the chicken with a slotted spoon and set aside. Skim any scum from the top of the poaching liquid.

2.  Bring the cooking liquid back to the boil. Add the rice. Reduce the heat and simmer, covered, for 15 minutes or until tender.

3.  Meanwhile, cut the corn kernels from the cob. Add the kernels and mushrooms to the soup and simmer for 1 minute or until tender.

4.  Meanwhile, shred the chicken into bite-sized pieces. Add the chicken, silverbeet and spring onion to the pan and cook until heated through and the silverbeet is bright green.

TIPS
You could add a bunch of asparagus to this soup when in season. Trim, cut into bite-sized pieces and add in step 3 with the corn (377 cal per serve).

If you prefer a different superfood, you can easily substitute kale or spinach for the silverbeet.

Tofu is a great, versatile alternative to meat. It's got heaps of protein and is packed with calcium, making it protective of your bones. Not only that, it contains plenty of omega-3s as well, helping your brain function. We should all be eating less meat, for the sake of the planet, but if anyone says to you that a meal's not a meal without meat, serve them this.

# Tofu stir-fry

1. Heat a wok over high heat. Stir-fry the snake beans for 3 minutes or until lightly charred. Add 2 tablespoons water and cook, covered, over medium heat for 2 minutes or until just tender and bright green. Set aside.

2. Heat half the oil in the same wok over high heat. Stir-fry the mushrooms for 2 minutes or until tender. Stir the garlic through and set aside with the beans.

3. Place the five-spice in a shallow dish. Add the tofu and toss to coat. Heat the remaining oil in the same wok. Stir-fry the tofu for 3 minutes or until golden. Return the beans and mushroom mixture to the wok with the cabbage and soy sauce. Stir-fry for 2 minutes or until well coated and the cabbage starts to soften. Serve with the steamed rice alongside.

TIP
Use green beans if you can't find any snake beans.

SERVES 2
PREP 15 minutes
COOK 15 minutes
CAL PER SERVE 304

150 g snake beans, cut into chunks
2 teaspoons peanut oil
100 g shiitake **mushrooms**
2 garlic cloves, crushed
3 teaspoons Chinese five-spice
300 g firm tofu, drained and
    cut into cubes
150 g green **cabbage**, finely
    shredded
2 teaspoons soy sauce
1 cup steamed rice

There is a lot going on in this dish . . . but with so few calories. Almonds, with all their mineral-y goodness, work really well with the fennel. And kangaroo is so low in fat that it makes the perfect stir-fry meat.

# Kangaroo, fennel & broccolini stir-fry

SERVES 2
PREP 15 minutes
COOK 15 minutes
CAL PER SERVE 349

2 tablespoons chopped raw
    almonds
1 bunch **broccolini**, trimmed
    and cut into chunks
2 teaspoons peanut oil
1 fennel bulb, trimmed and
    thinly sliced
3 garlic cloves, thinly sliced
250 g **kangaroo** fillet, trimmed
    and thickly sliced
1 tablespoon hoisin sauce

1. Heat a wok on medium–high. Cook the almonds for 3 minutes or until toasted. Set aside.

2. Heat the wok again on medium–high. Stir-fry the broccolini for 2 minutes or until lightly charred. Add 2 tablespoons water and cook, covered, for 2 minutes or until the water has evaporated and the broccolini is bright green and just tender. Set aside.

3. Heat half the oil in the same wok on medium–high. Stir-fry the fennel and garlic for 5 minutes or until golden and tender. Remove from the wok.

4. Heat the remaining oil in the wok over high heat. Stir-fry the kangaroo, in two batches, for 1 minute or until browned.

5. Return the broccolini, fennel and garlic to the wok with the hoisin sauce. Stir-fry until heated through. Serve sprinkled with the almonds.

TIP
You can use broccoli instead of broccolini.

VARIATION
You could stir through 100 g baby spinach and add a chopped long fresh red chilli just before serving (363 cal per serve).

Let's go green. With silverbeet and brussels sprouts, this recipe gives you loads of those nutrients that green vegetables abound in, such as vitamins A, C and K. The quick cooking of a stir-fry ensures that the vegies retain the maximum nutritional value when they hit your plate.

# Beef, sprouts & silverbeet stir-fry

1. Cut the silverbeet leaves from the stems. Discard the main white vein from the leaves and coarsely shred the remaining leaf. Thinly slice the stems, keeping them separate from the leaves.

2. Heat 1 teaspoon of the oil in a wok on high. Stir-fry the brussels sprouts for 4 minutes or until lightly charred. Add ⅓ cup (80 ml) water and cook, covered, on medium for 5 minutes or until bright green and tender crisp. Set aside.

3. Wipe the wok clean. Add the remaining oil to the wok and heat on high. Stir-fry the garlic for 1 minute or until crisp. Remove with a slotted spoon. Stir-fry the beef in two batches for 1 minute per batch or until browned. Set aside.

4. Stir-fry the silverbeet stems for 2 minutes or until golden. Return the beef and garlic to the wok with the leaves, sprouts and sauces. Stir-fry for 1 minute or until the leaves have just wilted. Serve sprinkled with the chilli.

TIP
The silverbeet lets out quite a bit of moisture. When cooked, transfer the stir-fry to a serving dish with a pair of tongs and bring the cooking liquid left in the wok to the boil. Boil for 1 minute or until thickened, then drizzle over the stir-fry. That way you get an amazing concentration of flavour.

SERVES 2
PREP 15 minutes
COOK 15 minutes
CAL PER SERVE 366

½ bunch **silverbeet**, trimmed
   and washed
3 teaspoons peanut oil
400 g **brussels sprouts**, halved
4 garlic cloves, thinly sliced
250 g **grass-fed beef**, trimmed
   of fat and cut into 1 cm slices
2 tablespoons oyster sauce
2 teaspoons soy sauce
1 long fresh red chilli, thinly sliced

Brown rice has a much higher nutritional content than its white counterpart, and its slightly nutty flavour combines well with the other ingredients in this dish. Make sure your tomatoes are nice and ripe to give the hint of sweetness that balances the salty cheese.

# Minted brown rice salad

SERVES 2
PREP 10 minutes
COOK 40 minutes
CAL PER SERVE 370

½ cup (100 g) brown rice
1 bunch **asparagus**, trimmed
    and cut into bite-sized chunks
200 g cherry **tomatoes**, halved
50 g low-cal fetta cheese, crumbled
¼ cup chopped fresh mint
2 spring onions, thinly sliced
3 teaspoons white-wine vinegar
1 tablespoon extra-virgin olive oil
freshly ground black pepper

1. Cook the rice in a small saucepan of boiling water for 40 minutes or until tender. Drain and allow to cool.

2. Meanwhile, blanch the asparagus in a small saucepan of boiling water for 1 minute or until bright green. Drain and cool in iced water. Drain.

3. Combine all the ingredients in a serving bowl. Season with black pepper and toss to combine.

TIP
You can make double the quantity as this is a perfect lunch box meal for the next day.

One of my all-time favourite superfood salads, this gets lots of different flavours fizzing around your tastebuds. It feels substantial, with pumpkin and chickpeas, but the raspberries add a touch of light freshness. Perfectly balanced.

# Chickpea, pumpkin & cheese salad

SERVES 2
PREP 10 minutes
COOK 40 minutes
CAL PER SERVE 348

400 g Kent pumpkin, unpeeled,
   cut into 1-cm thick wedges
olive oil spray
50 g **raspberries**
2 teaspoons olive oil
2 teaspoons white-wine vinegar
freshly ground black pepper
80 g baby **spinach** leaves
400 g can **chickpeas**, drained
   and rinsed
80 g soft goat's cheese, crumbled

1. Preheat the oven to 200°C (180°C fan-forced). Line a baking tray with baking paper. Arrange the pumpkin in a single layer on the tray and lightly spray with oil. Bake for 40 minutes or until golden and tender. Set aside to cool to room temperature.

2. Meanwhile, crush the raspberries in a small bowl with a fork. Add the oil and vinegar and season with black pepper. Whisk until well combined.

3. Arrange the spinach leaves, pumpkin and chickpeas on a serving plate. Sprinkle the cheese over and drizzle with the raspberry dressing.

TIP
You can use fresh or frozen (thawed) raspberries for this recipe.

Beetroot makes a sublime addition to so many salads. Nowhere is that more true than here. The tartness of the vinegar and gherkin balance the sweetness of the baby beets. This salad is the perfect lunch, but is substantial enough to be a summer dinner, preferably eaten outside.

# Rare roast beef & beetroot salad

1. Steam the potatoes over a saucepan of boiling water for 15 minutes or until tender. Place in a large bowl.

2. Meanwhile, combine the vinegar, oil, shallot and gherkin in a small bowl. Season with black pepper. Drizzle over the hot potatoes and toss to coat. Allow to cool to room temperature.

3. Add the beetroot, roast beef and salad leaves. Gently toss to coat and season with black pepper.

TIPS

Tossing the potatoes through the dressing while still hot will make them absorb all the flavours. If packing for your lunch box, keep the mixed leaves separate to toss through just before eating.

You could also use desirée or kipfler potatoes.

SERVES 2
PREP 10 minutes, plus cooling
COOK 15 minutes
CAL PER SERVE 330

300 g baby carisma potatoes,
    halved
3 teaspoons white-wine vinegar
2 teaspoons extra-virgin olive oil
1 shallot, finely chopped
1 gherkin, finely chopped
freshly ground black pepper
450 g can whole baby **beetroot**,
    drained and halved
150 g thinly sliced rare roast beef,
    torn into bite-sized pieces
50 g mixed salad leaves

Roasting the beetroot brings out its sweetness, which means it goes well with the tarter tastes of ingredients like wine vinegar, and the peppery tang of rocket. I like to serve this outdoors on a warm spring day.

# Roasted beetroot salad

SERVES 2
PREP 15 minutes
COOK 1 hour
CAL PER SERVE 341

**600 g beetroot, trimmed,**
    **peeled and cut into chunks**
**3 garlic cloves, unpeeled**
**4 sprigs fresh thyme**
**freshly ground black pepper**
**olive oil spray**
**1 tablespoon red-wine vinegar**
**1 tablespoon extra-virgin olive oil**
**60 g baby rocket**
**100 g (3 balls) bocconcini cheese,**
    **drained and sliced**

1. Preheat the oven to 190°C (170°C fan-forced). Place the beetroot, garlic and thyme on a baking tray. Season with black pepper and lightly spray with olive oil. Roast for 1 hour or until tender.

2. Discard the thyme. Set aside the beetroot to cool slightly. Squeeze the flesh from the garlic and combine with the vinegar and oil in a small bowl.

3. Arrange the warm beetroot, rocket and bocconcini on a serving plate and drizzle with the dressing.

TIP
Roasted beetroot is great paired with nuts and cheeses such as fetta, soft goat's cheese or ricotta. You can also serve it as a side with roasted pork, chicken or beef.

Meat, potatoes and three veg . . . but a little different from the traditional meaning! The dressing for the potato salad is just divine, and with our superfood friend yoghurt providing the base, you avoid too much oil or cream, which can really up the calories.

# Tarragon chicken & potato salad

SERVES 2
PREP 15 minutes
COOK 15 minutes
CAL PER SERVE 380

300 g chicken breast, trimmed
300 g baby carisma potatoes, halved
1 bunch **broccolini**, trimmed and cut into chunks
1 bunch **asparagus**, trimmed and cut into chunks
1 celery stalk, trimmed and thinly sliced
2 tablespoons low-cal Greek-style **yoghurt**
1 teaspoon white-wine vinegar
1 teaspoon Dijon mustard
1 tablespoon chopped fresh tarragon
freshly ground black pepper

1. Place the chicken in a small saucepan and cover with water. Bring to the boil. Reduce the heat and simmer for 5 minutes. Remove from the heat and leave the chicken in the cooking liquid for 10 minutes to cook through. Remove the chicken from the liquid.

2. When cool enough to handle, shred the chicken. (Cool the chicken stock and refrigerate or freeze for another use.)

3. Meanwhile, steam the potatoes over a saucepan of boiling water for 15 minutes or until tender. Add the broccolini, asparagus and celery 3 minutes before the end of the cooking time. Drain and cool.

4. Combine the yoghurt, vinegar, mustard and tarragon in a large bowl. Season with black pepper. Add the vegetables and chicken and gently toss to coat.

TIPS
Use the chicken stock when making soup.

You could also use desirée or kipfler potatoes.

The tangy lemon flavour of sumac is one I've used in a couple of recipes in this book. Here it provides a perfect bridge between the citrus of the orange and the slightly sweet chicken (the light charring caramelises some of the natural sugars in the meat).

# Moroccan chicken salad

1. Preheat a char-grill pan on medium. Lightly spray the chicken with oil and sprinkle with the sumac. Cook for 8–10 minutes or until lightly charred and cooked through.

2. Meanwhile, arrange the spinach, orange segments and celery on a serving plate. Combine 2 teaspoons of the reserved orange juice with the oil and garlic in a small bowl.

3. Thickly slice the chicken and add to the salad. Sprinkle with the almonds and drizzle the dressing over to serve.

TIPS
See page 26 for how to segment an orange.

If packing for your lunch box, keep the dressing separate and add only when ready to serve.

SERVES 2
PREP 15 minutes
COOK 10 minutes
CAL PER SERVE 413

300 g chicken breast, trimmed
olive oil spray
1 teaspoon sumac
50 g baby **spinach** leaves
2 **oranges**, segmented, juice
   reserved
1 celery stalk, trimmed
   and thinly sliced
2 teaspoons extra-virgin olive oil
½ garlic clove, crushed
2 tablespoons chopped raw
   **almonds**

This is so quick to prepare – I love it. If asparagus is not in season, you can substitute some green beans. As a lunch, it's substantial, healthy, tasty and low in calories – what more could you ask for?

# Spicy kangaroo salad with chickpeas

1. Season the kangaroo with black pepper. Lightly spray a medium frying pan with oil and heat on high. Cook the kangaroo for 1 minute each side for rare or until cooked to your liking. Set aside to rest.

2. Blanch the asparagus in a small saucepan of boiling water for 1 minute or until bright green. Drain and cool in iced water. Drain.

3. Combine the vinegar, oil and chilli in a small bowl.

4. Thickly slice the kangaroo. Place the chickpeas, mixed leaves, capsicum and asparagus in a medium bowl. Drizzle with the dressing and toss to coat. Arrange on a serving plate and top with the kangaroo slices.

TIP
If packing for a lunch box, wait until the kangaroo is cool and pack the dressing separately.

SERVES 2
PREP 15 minutes
COOK 5 minutes
CAL PER SERVE 376

250 g **kangaroo** fillet, trimmed
freshly ground black pepper
olive oil spray
1 bunch **asparagus**, trimmed
    and cut into chunks
1 tablespoon red-wine vinegar
1 tablespoon extra-virgin olive oil
½ long fresh red chilli, finely
    chopped
400 g can **chickpeas**, drained
    and rinsed
60 g mixed salad leaves
1 small red capsicum, thinly sliced

An awesome way to use leftover chicken. The trio of lemon juice, sesame oil and coriander combined with fresh vegetables gives an invigorating zing to this dish.

# Asian chicken coleslaw

SERVES 2
PREP 15 minutes
CAL PER SERVE 313

**300 g leftover skinless soy chicken
(see page 100), shredded**
**250 g brussels sprouts,
thinly shredded**
**½ green capsicum, finely sliced**
**2 spring onions, finely chopped**
**½ cup coarsely chopped fresh
coriander**
**2 teaspoons lemon juice**
**1 teaspoon sesame oil**
**freshly ground black pepper**

1. Place all the ingredients in a large bowl. Season with black pepper and toss to combine.

TIPS
Use a mandoline to shred the brussels sprouts. It will be done faster and the result will be as light as air.

You can make this salad with any cooked chicken you have at hand – simply add ½–1 tablespoon soy sauce according to taste when tossing the ingredients together.

VARIATION
Replace the capsicum with a medium thinly sliced unpeeled red apple and add 40 g shredded baby spinach (348 cal per serve).

This is one of the best ways of cooking meat. Quick and easy, while avoiding too much oil, it also gives a hint of smokiness to the beef. And with such an array of vegetables, you can't go wrong with this dish.

# Chinese beef skewers

SERVES 2
PREP 15 minutes
COOK 10 minutes
CAL PER SERVE 362

1 teaspoon ground cumin
3 garlic cloves, crushed
2 teaspoons peanut oil
300 g grass-fed beef rump steak,
    trimmed and cut into 3 cm pieces
freshly ground black pepper
115 g baby corn, halved
1 bunch **broccoli**, cut into florets
100 g green beans, halved
100 g snow peas, halved on
    the diagonal

1. Place the cumin, a third of the garlic and half the oil in a shallow dish. Add the beef, season with black pepper and toss to coat. Thread the beef onto four metal skewers.

2. Heat the remaining oil in a wok on high. Stir-fry the corn, broccoli and beans for 2 minutes. Reduce the heat to medium, add 2 tablespoons water and stir-fry, covered, for 5 minutes until the vegetables are just tender and the water has evaporated. Add the snow peas and remaining garlic and stir-fry for 1 minute.

3. Meanwhile, heat a char-grill pan on medium–high. Cook the beef, turning once, for 2–3 minutes for medium–rare or until cooked to your liking. Serve with the stir-fried vegetables alongside.

TIP
If using bamboo skewers, soak them in cold water for 30 minutes before threading the meat to avoid them burning.

Alongside the superfood duo of mushrooms and yoghurt, this recipe also features red onion. The humble onion actually has some important nutritional content to offer, particularly anti-inflammatories and antioxidants. This is a great dish to share, and it's easy to up the quantities. I just serve everything in the centre of the table and let everyone help themselves.

# Middle Eastern lamb skewers

SERVES 2
PREP 15 minutes
COOK 10 minutes
CAL PER SERVE 360

260 g lamb fillet, trimmed
   and cut into 3 cm cubes
1 small red capsicum, cut
   into 3 cm chunks
1 small red onion, cut
   into 3 cm chunks
1 zucchini, cut into ½ cm slices
4 baby **mushrooms**
olive oil spray
2 teaspoons sumac
freshly ground black pepper
⅔ cup (190 g) low-cal Greek-style
   **yoghurt**
2 teaspoons tahini
1 garlic clove, crushed

1. Thread the lamb, capsicum, onion and zucchini alternately onto four metal skewers. Finish each skewer with a mushroom. Lightly spray with oil. Sprinkle with the sumac and season with black pepper.

2. Heat a char-grill pan or barbecue flat plate on medium–high. Cook the lamb skewers, turning, for 6 minutes for medium–rare or until cooked to your liking.

3. Meanwhile, combine the yoghurt, tahini and garlic in a small bowl.

4. Serve the skewers with the yoghurt dipping sauce alongside.

TIP
This yoghurt sauce is also great with grilled meat or fish and steamed seasonal vegetables.

There are few better ways to mark the turn of the season from winter to spring than this dish. Lots of crisp, young vegetables – including superfood asparagus with all its vitamin K and other nutrients – that are given a twist by the addition of mint.

# Lamb cutlets with spring vegetables

1. Heat the oil in a large saucepan over medium heat. Cook the onion, turning, for 5 minutes or until golden. Add the carrots and stock and bring to the boil. Reduce the heat to medium–low and simmer, covered, for 5 minutes. Add the broccolini and asparagus and simmer, covered, for 5 minutes. Stir in the mint and season with black pepper.

2. Meanwhile, lightly spray a non-stick frying pan with oil and heat on medium–high. Cook the lamb cutlets for 2–3 minutes each side for medium–rare or until cooked to your liking.

3. Serve the cutlets with the spring vegetables alongside.

TIP
You can use broccoli instead of broccolini.

SERVES 2
PREP 15 minutes
COOK 15 minutes
CAL PER SERVE 380

**1 teaspoon olive oil**
**4 spring onions, trimmed,**
    **leaving 5 cm stalks**
**1 bunch baby carrots, trimmed,**
    **leaving 2 cm stalks**
**⅓ cup (80 ml) low-sodium**
    **chicken stock**
**1 bunch broccolini, trimmed**
    **and cut into 5 cm pieces**
**1 bunch asparagus, trimmed**
    **and cut into 5 cm pieces**
**2 tablespoons chopped fresh mint**
**freshly ground black pepper**
**olive oil spray**
**6 frenched lamb cutlets, trimmed**

There's so much going on in this sandwich, it makes my mouth water just thinking about it. All the flavours balance really well. Perfect for making the day before for lunch boxes, a picnic or a casual gathering with friends.

# Rare roast beef & pesto bun

MAKES 2
PREP 15 minutes
COOK 10 minutes
CAL PER SERVE 304

**1 large red capsicum, quartered and deseeded**
**2 wholemeal bread buns (150 g)**
**50 g silken firm tofu, drained**
**⅓ cup fresh basil leaves**
**1 small garlic clove, crushed**
**2 tablespoons finely grated parmesan cheese**
**freshly ground black pepper**
**80 g rare roast beef, torn into bite-sized pieces**
**½ cup baby spinach leaves**

1. Place the capsicum skin-side up on an oven tray. Place under a preheated grill for 8 minutes or until charred. Transfer to a bowl with a lid and set aside, covered, for 10 minutes to cool.

2. Meanwhile, cut a shallow lid from the top of each bun. Remove the soft bread inside, leaving a thick shell.

3. To make the pesto, place the tofu, basil, garlic and parmesan in a food processor and process until smooth. Season with black pepper.

4. Drain the capsicum. Remove and discard the skin.

5. Spread the base inside each bun with half of the pesto. Layer with half the capsicum then the beef, pressing down. Spread the remaining pesto over the top, add the spinach and finish with a layer of capsicum, pressing down firmly. Replace the bread lid. Wrap each bun in plastic wrap and refrigerate for at least 4 hours. Remove from the fridge and bring to room temperature to serve.

TIP
Process the soft bread from the inside of the buns and store in a zip-lock bag in the freezer for breadcrumbs.

VARIATION
Use rocket leaves instead of basil for a peppery pesto.

Prawns are damn close to being a superfood in their own right. They combine oodles of protein with low levels of fat, making them healthy and quick to cook. Prawns also contain lots of iron, which is good for your blood. They are great for sharing, and you can use the tails to eat them – go on, get your hands dirty!

# Chilli garlic prawns

SERVES 2
PREP 15 minutes
COOK 10 minutes
CAL PER SERVE 299

1 bunch **asparagus**, trimmed
   and cut into chunks
80 g baby **spinach** leaves
2 teaspoons olive oil
600 g medium king prawns,
   peeled and deveined,
   tails intact
3 garlic cloves, thinly sliced
½ long fresh red chilli, finely
   chopped
1 tablespoon lemon juice
2 slices wholemeal sourdough,
   toasted

**1.** Cook the asparagus in a small saucepan of boiling water for 2 minutes or until just tender. Drain and cool in iced water. Drain. Arrange the spinach and asparagus on two serving plates.

**2.** Heat the oil in a large frying pan over medium–high heat. Cook the prawns for 3 minutes. Add the garlic and chilli and cook, stirring, for another 3 minutes or until the prawns are pink and lightly charred. Add the lemon juice and toss to coat.

**3.** Top the salad with the prawns and any pan juices. Serve with the toasted sourdough alongside.

VARIATION
Try this dish with 300 g cleaned baby octopus instead of prawns (351 cal per serve). Make sure your pan is very hot before adding them so they sear and don't stew.

A taste of India for an autumnal lunch. The spices form a delicious crust on the fish that you break through into the succulent flesh beneath.

# Indian fish with beetroot raita

1. Combine the yoghurt, beetroot and onion in a small bowl. Season with black pepper.

2. Coarsely grind the fennel and coriander seeds in a mortar and pestle. Place in a shallow dish with the remaining spices. Season with black pepper. Add the fish and turn to coat.

3. Steam the brussels sprouts over a saucepan of boiling water for 5–6 minutes or until just tender.

4. Meanwhile, heat the oil in a non-stick frying pan over medium–high heat. Cook the fish for 3–5 minutes each side or until golden and just cooked through.

5. Serve the fish with the sprouts and beetroot raita alongside.

TIPS
Don't forget your plastic gloves to prepare the beetroot.

This raita looks stunning and is great with vegetable sticks as an aperitif with friends (172 cal for the raita).

VARIATION
Make this dish with a salmon fillet instead (415 cal per serve).

SERVES 2
PREP 20 minutes
COOK 10 minutes
CAL PER SERVE 317

½ cup (140 g) no-fat Greek-style
   yoghurt
150 g **beetroot**, peeled
   and coarsely grated
1 spring onion, trimmed
   and finely chopped
freshly ground black pepper
1 teaspoon fennel seeds
1 teaspoon coriander seeds
1 teaspoon ground turmeric
1 teaspoon ground cumin
2 x 150 g skinless blue-eye
   trevalla fillets
400 g **brussels sprouts**, halved
2 teaspoons vegetable oil

Fruit, nuts and fish – it might seem a bit of a strange combination, but don't be put off; I assure you that this salad tastes sublime. Lots of superfoods, bags of flavour and easy to prepare – that makes it pretty special in my book.

# Hot-smoked salmon salad

SERVES 2
PREP 15 minutes
CAL PER SERVE 372

**2 teaspoons white-wine vinegar**
**1 teaspoon Dijon mustard**
**1 teaspoon extra-virgin olive oil**
**2 oranges, segmented,**
   **juice reserved (see page 28)**
**150 g hot-smoked salmon,**
   **skin removed and**
   **flesh flaked**
**60 g endive, sliced**
**½ Pink Lady apple, cored**
   **and thinly sliced**
**¼ cup (25 g) walnuts, chopped**
**freshly ground black pepper**

1. Combine the vinegar, mustard, oil and 2 teaspoons reserved orange juice in a small bowl.

2. Place the salmon, endive, orange segments, apple and walnuts in a large bowl. Add the dressing and gently toss to coat. Season with black pepper.

TIP
If you have any leftover smoked salmon, pop it into a sandwich for your lunch box the next day.

VARIATION
You could replace the oranges with 1 large ruby grapefruit and the walnuts with raw almonds (323 cal per serve).

Tuna is glorious. It didn't quite make my superfoods list, but I still thoroughly recommend you get some into your diet as it's full of omega-3 oils, vitamins and protein. It really lends itself to marinating – the subtle taste of the flesh combines with the marinade to delicious effect. Just make sure your tuna comes from a sustainable source.

# Grilled tuna with soba noodle salad

SERVES 2
PREP 20 minutes
COOK 10 minutes
CAL PER SERVE 396

2 tablespoons light soy sauce
2 teaspoons finely grated
   fresh ginger
2 teaspoons sesame oil
250 g sashimi-grade tuna
olive oil spray
3 teaspoons white-wine vinegar
2 teaspoons mirin
70 g dried soba noodles
100 g green **cabbage**, finely
   shredded
100 g snow peas, finely shredded
1 spring onion, thinly sliced
½ cup chopped fresh coriander
freshly ground black pepper

1. Combine the soy sauce, ginger and half the sesame oil in a shallow dish. Add the tuna and turn to coat. Refrigerate for 15 minutes, turning every 5 minutes to evenly marinate.

2. Lightly spray a barbecue flat plate with oil and heat on high. Remove the tuna from the marinade and place on the flat plate. Grill for 1 minute each side. Remove from the barbecue and set aside to cool to room temperature.

3. Meanwhile, combine the vinegar, mirin and remaining sesame oil in a small bowl.

4. Cook the noodles in a saucepan of boiling water for 4 minutes or until just tender. Drain, cool under cold running water and drain again. Place in a large bowl with the dressing and the remaining ingredients. Season with black pepper and toss to coat. Thickly slice the tuna and serve with the soba noodle salad alongside.

VARIATION
Make this salad with salmon instead of tuna (383 cal per serve) and add 40 g shredded baby spinach leaves (387 cal per serve).

I love this recipe as a weekend lunch, but it also works as a dish to share with friends in front of a movie. You can also pop some in your lunch box for the next day. Toasting the pine nuts really brings out their flavour.

# Pumpkin & tomato pide

SERVES 2
PREP 20 minutes
COOK 25 minutes
CAL PER SERVE 328

250 g pumpkin, peeled and cut into thin wedges
olive oil spray
½ cup (140 g) no-fat natural yoghurt
2 teaspoons lemon juice
½ garlic clove, crushed
freshly ground black pepper
1 Lebanese cucumber, sliced
¼ small red onion, thinly sliced
1 (100 g) flat round wholemeal lite Lebanese bread
1 tablespoon low-sodium tomato paste
1 teaspoon za'atar
100 g grape tomatoes, halved
1 tablespoon pine nuts, toasted
2 tablespoons fresh mint leaves, torn

1. Preheat oven to 220°C (200°C fan-forced). Line a baking tray with baking paper.

2. Arrange the pumpkin in a single layer on the baking tray and lightly spray with oil. Roast for 15 minutes or until tender.

3. Meanwhile, combine the yoghurt, lemon juice and garlic in a small bowl. Season with black pepper. Arrange the cucumber and onion on a serving plate.

4. Spread the bread with tomato paste and sprinkle with za'atar.

5. Increase the oven to 235°C (215°C fan-forced). Place the bread on the hot tray used to cook the pumpkin. Arrange the pumpkin and tomatoes on the bread and bake for 5–8 minutes or until the base of the bread is crisp.

6. Sprinkle with the pine nuts and mint leaves and drizzle with the garlic yoghurt. Serve with the cucumber and onion alongside.

sardine

tomatoes

broccoli

cranberrie

almonds

*SUPER* DINNER

beet

eggs

mushrooms

chickpeas

troot

yoghur

cabbage

Just look at the colour of this soup! And it not only looks amazing, it's good for you too! All these earthy vegetables give lots of vitamins and minerals, while garlic – which is good for your blood – is in there as well.

# Root vegetable soup

SERVES 4
PREP 15 minutes
COOK 35 minutes
CALS PER SERVE 321

**1 tablespoon olive oil**
**1 onion, chopped**
**500 g desirée potatoes, peeled and diced**
**400 g beetroot, peeled and diced**
**400 g parsnip, peeled and diced**
**400 g carrot, peeled and chopped**
**300 g turnip, peeled and diced**
**3 garlic cloves, crushed**
**1 L low-sodium vegetable stock**
**freshly ground black pepper**

1. Heat the oil in a large saucepan on medium–high. Cook the onion for 5 minutes or until softened. Add the potato, beetroot, parsnip, carrot and turnip and cook for 5 minutes. Stir in the garlic and cook for 30 seconds. Add the stock and 1 cup (250 ml) water. Bring to the boil. Reduce the heat and simmer, covered, for 20 minutes or until the vegetables are tender. Season with black pepper.

TIPS
Cut all your vegetables to approximately the same size so they cook evenly.

Freeze the cooled soup in airtight containers for up to one month.

Just the one superfood in this recipe, but so many other good things alongside it. The mixture of peas and beans gives heaps of fibre and iron, while the chicken gives a meaty texture without overloading the calorie count. Add the delicious dressing and you've got one hell of a tasty salad.

# Chicken salad with beans & peas

SERVES 2
PREP 15 minutes
COOK 10 minutes
CAL PER SERVE 380

**250 g skinless chicken breast, trimmed**
**freshly ground black pepper**
**olive oil spray**
**100 g green beans, trimmed**
**100 g snow peas, trimmed**
**½ cup (60 g) frozen peas**
**¼ cup (70 g) no-fat Greek-style yoghurt**
**¼ cup fresh mint leaves**
**½ garlic clove**
**400 g can cannellini beans, drained and rinsed**

1. Season the chicken with black pepper. Lightly spray a char-grill pan with olive oil and heat on medium–high. Cook the chicken for 4–5 minutes each side or until lightly charred and cooked through.

2. Meanwhile, cook the green beans in a medium saucepan of boiling water for 4 minutes, adding the snow peas and frozen peas for the last 2 minutes. Drain and cool in iced water. Drain.

3. Process the yoghurt, mint and garlic together until smooth.

4. Thickly slice the chicken. Arrange the beans, peas and chicken on a serving plate. Drizzle with the dressing.

The Asian flavours in this recipe are just mouth-watering – that whole sweet-and-sour thing really takes it up a notch. Ginger is a very useful ingredient for exercise as it is anti-inflammatory.

# Chinese soy chicken

SERVES 4
PREP 10 minutes
COOK 1 hour
CAL PER SERVE 387

1.5 kg whole chicken, trimmed
4 spring onions, chopped into
   8 cm lengths, plus extra,
   shredded, to serve
2 cm piece fresh ginger, sliced
1 cup (250 ml) dark soy sauce
1 cup (250 ml) light soy sauce
1 cup (250 ml) shaoxing
   (Chinese rice wine) or
   dry sherry
¼ cup (55 g) brown sugar
3 whole star anise
2 cinnamon sticks
2 bunches **gai lan (Chinese
   broccoli)**
coriander leaves, to serve

## Ginger sauce

1 tablespoon peanut oil
1 tablespoon grated fresh ginger
4 spring onions, finely chopped

1.  Remove any visible fat from the chicken and wipe with paper towel to remove any blood and surface moisture.

2.  Place 4 cups (1 L) water, the spring onion, ginger, soy sauces, shaoxing, sugar, star anise and cinnamon in a large saucepan. Stir until the sugar has dissolved. Add the chicken, breast-side down and heat on medium. Slowly bring to the boil. Reduce the heat, cover and simmer for 10 minutes. Without lifting the lid, remove from the heat and stand, covered, for 45 minutes to finish cooking.

3.  Meanwhile, to make the ginger sauce, heat the oil in a small saucepan on high. Stir in the ginger and spring onion and remove from the heat. Set aside to cool.

4.  Remove the chicken from the saucepan, draining well, and place on a board. Cut into serving-sized pieces and arrange on a serving platter.

5.  Steam the gai lan over a saucepan of boiling water for 3–4 minutes or until just tender.

6.  Spoon ⅓ cup hot poaching liquid over the chicken and garnish with the spring onion and coriander. Serve with the ginger sauce and steamed gai lan alongside.

TIP
Leave the skin on to poach as it helps keep the chicken moist, but don't waste your precious calories eating the skin. Cool and freeze the poaching liquid for another use.

Time to tang it up! Cajun spice mix comes in a variety of strengths, so you can choose one that suits your taste for hotness. This is a real hands-on meal and is very adaptable to whatever meat you have to hand.

# Mexican chicken skewers

SERVES 2
PREP 15 minutes
COOK 10 minutes
CAL PER SERVE 393

**300 g chicken breast, trimmed and cut into 3 cm cubes**
**2 teaspoons Cajun spice mix**
**olive oil spray**
**1 large corncob**
**125 g can chickpeas, drained and rinsed**
**1 green capsicum, diced**
**2 Roma tomatoes, diced**
**¼ cup chopped fresh coriander**
**2 teaspoons lemon juice**
**2 teaspoons extra-virgin olive oil**
**1 garlic clove, crushed**
**freshly ground black pepper**

1. Sprinkle the chicken with the spice mix and thread onto four metal skewers.

2. Lightly spray a char-grill pan with oil and heat on medium. Cook the chicken, turning, for 8–10 minutes or until lightly charred and cooked through.

3. Meanwhile, microwave the corn in a microwave-proof dish, covered, on high (100 per cent) for 2 minutes or until just tender. Cook alongside the chicken for 3 minutes or until lightly charred.

4. Meanwhile, combine the chickpeas, capsicum, tomato, coriander, lemon juice, oil and garlic in a medium bowl. Season with black pepper and toss to coat.

5. Cut the corn into chunks and serve with the chicken skewers and the salsa.

VARIATION
Make this dish with kangaroo fillet (338 cal per serve) or salmon (403 calories per serve) instead of chicken.

Who doesn't love a beef and mushroom pie? This one is made extra 'super' with the addition of calves' liver, giving another taste and texture – as well as all its nutrients. And, believe me, the smell of these beauties as they are cooking in the oven . . . heavenly!

# Express beef & calves' liver pie

1. Preheat the oven to 200°C (180°C fan-forced).

2. Heat 1 teaspoon oil in a large frying pan on high. Cook the liver and steak for 1 minute or until browned. Set aside and thickly slice.

3. Heat 1 teaspoon oil in the same pan and cook the mushrooms, stirring, for 4 minutes or until browned. Set aside.

4. Heat 1 teaspoon oil in the same pan on medium and cook the onion and thyme, stirring, for 5 minutes or until the onion is softened.

5. Whisk the stock, cornflour and tomato paste together in a jug until smooth. Return the mushrooms to the pan with the stock mixture and bring to the boil. Reduce the heat to medium and simmer for 2 minutes or until thickened. Stir in the meat. Spoon the mixture into two 1½-cup (325 ml) shallow ovenproof ramekins.

6. Lightly spray one sheet of pastry with oil and top with the second sheet. Lightly spray with oil and fold over twice to form a 14 cm x 22 cm rectangle. Cut in half to obtain two 11 cm x 14 cm rectangles.

7. Top the filling with the prepared pastry, slightly tucking the edges into the ramekin. Lightly spray with oil and sprinkle with paprika. Bake for 18 minutes or until the pastry is golden and crisp and the filling is bubbling hot.

8. Serve the pies with the mixed leaves drizzled with the vinegar and remaining oil.

TIP
Double this recipe for a delicious winter meal with friends.

SERVES 2
PREP 15 minutes
COOK 30 minutes
CALS PER SERVE 366

**4 teaspoons olive oil**
**150 g calves' liver**
**100 g rump steak, trimmed**
**200 g mushrooms, chopped**
**1 brown onion, finely chopped**
**2 teaspoons fresh thyme leaves**
**1 cup (250 ml) low-sodium beef stock**
**1 tablespoon cornflour**
**1 tablespoon low-sodium tomato paste**
**olive oil spray**
**2 sheets filo pastry**
**smoked paprika, to sprinkle**
**50 g mixed salad leaves**
**2 teaspoons balsamic vinegar**

I'm a big fan of fruit in salads, and this one is deliciously different. Sweet and salty flavours combine in the dressing, while the pineapple and the tomatoes jostle together among the salad leaves. A lovely, distinctive accompaniment to a steak.

# Grilled steak with pineapple salad

SERVES 2
PREP 10 minutes
COOK 8 minutes
CAL PER SERVE 311

**300 g grass-fed beef scotch fillet,**
    **trimmed**
**freshly ground black pepper**
**2 teaspoons olive oil**
**1 long fresh red chilli, seeded,**
    **finely chopped**
**1 garlic clove, crushed**
**2 teaspoons lime juice**
**2 teaspoons fish sauce**
**2 teaspoons brown sugar**
**70 g Asian mixed salad leaves**
**300 g fresh pineapple, peeled,**
    **cored and cut into wedges**
**100 g cherry tomatoes, halved**
**2 tablespoons torn fresh mint**
    **leaves**
**2 tablespoons torn fresh**
    **Thai basil leaves**

1. Season the beef with black pepper. Heat half the oil in a frying pan on high. Cook the beef for 1–2 minutes each side for medium–rare or until cooked to your liking.

2. Meanwhile, combine the chilli, garlic, lime juice, fish sauce and sugar in a small bowl. Arrange the mixed leaves, pineapple and tomatoes on a serving plate. Drizzle with the dressing and sprinkle the herbs over the top.

3. Cut the fillet in half and serve with the pineapple salad alongside.

TIP
If you've done a big workout serve this dish with ½ cup cooked rice, adding 107 cal.

VARIATION
You can serve this salad with 300 g grilled skinless chicken breast instead of beef (314 cal per serve).

This is a great way to cook calves' liver, and ideal for those trying this true superfood for the first time. Sweet potato is an awesome provider of antioxidants and vitamin C.

# Calves' liver with sweet potato bake

1. Preheat the oven to 170°C (150°C fan-forced).

2. Heat the milk and garlic together in a small saucepan over medium heat until almost boiling. Season with black pepper and set aside to infuse.

3. Heat the oil in a large frying pan on medium–high. Cook the onion, stirring, for 5 minutes or until softened. Layer the sweet potato and onion in two 1-cup (250 ml) ovenproof dishes. Strain the milk over the vegetables and cover with foil. Bake for 45 minutes. Discard the foil and sprinkle with the cheese. Bake for another 10 minutes or until golden.

4. Meanwhile, lightly spray a char-grill pan with oil and heat on medium–high. Season the liver with black pepper and cook for 2 minutes each side for medium–rare or until cooked to your liking.

5. Serve the liver with the onion and sweet potato bake.

TIPS

Use a mandoline to slice the sweet potato as thinly as possible. You may need to order the calves' liver from your butcher, as they don't always carry this item.

The cooking time for the liver will depend on the thickness of the piece. Try not to overcook it or it will become tough.

The finer you grate the cheese the more bountiful it will seem.

SERVES 2
PREP 15 minutes
COOK 1 hour
CAL PER SERVE 407

¾ cup (180 ml) low-cal milk
2 garlic cloves, bruised
freshly ground black pepper
1 teaspoon olive oil
1 large onion, thinly sliced
280 g sweet potato, peeled and very thinly sliced
10 g low-cal cheddar cheese, finely grated
olive oil spray
275 g calves' liver
mixed salad leaves, to serve

Is there a better winter warmer than a chilli con carne? I serve this dish with one of my top superfoods alongside, but the tomatoes within are also a dose of super goodness.

# Chunky chilli con carne

SERVES 6
PREP 10 minutes
COOK 1 hour 50 minutes
CAL PER SERVE 364

**600 g grass-fed gravy beef,**
**trimmed and cut into**
**4 cm pieces**
**freshly ground black pepper**
**2 teaspoons olive oil**
**2 red capsicums, thinly sliced**
**1 onion, chopped**
**4 garlic cloves, crushed**
**1 tablespoon ground cumin**
**2 teaspoons ground coriander**
**½ teaspoon dried chilli flakes**
**1 x 400 g can diced tomatoes**
**1¼ cups (310 ml) low-sodium**
**beef stock**
**1 tablespoon low-sodium**
**tomato paste**
**2 teaspoons dried oregano**
**3 x 400 g cans red kidney beans,**
**drained and rinsed**
**1 bunch silverbeet leaves,**
**leaves picked, washed and**
**coarsely chopped**
**1 cup (280 g) no-fat Greek-style**
**yoghurt**
**½ cup fresh coriander sprigs**

1. Preheat the oven to 200°C (180°C fan-forced).

2. Season the beef with black pepper. Heat the oil in a large non-stick saucepan on medium–high. Cook the beef, in two batches, for 4 minutes or until well browned. Set aside. Reduce the heat to medium. Cook the capsicum, stirring, for 5 minutes and set aside. Cook the onion in the same pan, stirring, for 5 minutes or until softened. Stir in the garlic and spices and cook, stirring, for 30 seconds or until fragrant. Return the beef to the pan with the tomatoes, stock, tomato paste and oregano and bring to the boil. Cook in the oven, covered, for 30 minutes. Add the beans and cook for another 30 minutes. Stir in the capsicum and cook for 30 minutes or until the beef is very tender.

3. Meanwhile, steam the silverbeet leaves over a saucepan of boiling water for 3 minutes or until wilted and bright green.

4. Add a dollop of yoghurt to the chilli con carne and sprinkle with the coriander. Serve with the silverbeet alongside.

TIPS
Once cooled, you can freeze this dish in airtight containers for up to one month.

When browning meat in batches, don't heat all the oil at the beginning, as you will need to add more to the pan for the last batch.

Okay, it might be a bit controversial to serve a burger without a bun, but believe me, when you taste this you won't miss the bread. The two types of potato wedges are the perfect accompaniment.

# Open beef burger with beetroot relish

SERVES 2
PREP 15 minutes
COOK 35 minutes
CAL PER SERVE 405

200 g potato, cut into wedges

200 g sweet potato, cut into wedges

freshly ground black pepper

olive oil spray

1 small onion, finely chopped

200 g grass-fed beef mince

2 tablespoons finely chopped fresh flat-leaf parsley

2 tablespoons **beetroot** relish

2 **eggs**

mixed salad leaves, to serve

1. Preheat the oven to 200°C (180°C fan-forced). Line an oven tray with baking paper. Arrange both types of potato, in a single layer, on the tray. Season with black pepper and lightly spray with oil. Roast for 35 minutes, turning halfway through.

2. Meanwhile, lightly spray a non-stick frying pan with oil and heat on medium. Cook the onion, stirring, for 3 minutes or until softened. Set aside to cool.

3. Combine the onion, beef, parsley and half the relish in a bowl. Divide in half and shape each portion into a 9-cm wide patty.

4. Lightly spray the frying pan with oil again and heat on medium. Cook the patties for 4–5 minutes each side for medium–rare or until cooked to your liking. Set aside, loosely covered with foil to keep warm.

5. Wipe the pan clean and lightly spray with oil. Heat on high. Crack the eggs into the pan and cook for 2–3 minutes for the white to set or until cooked to your liking.

6. Top the patties with the remaining relish and egg. Serve with the wedges and salad leaves alongside.

TIP
You can make a double batch of patties and freeze half.

Pig farming used to have some of the worst practices in food production. Things have improved, but for the most humanely-reared meat you need to choose organic, free-range pork whenever possible. Caraway seeds have quite a strong flavour, so you don't need to use that many of them. But even with a small amount, you get good levels of fibre and antioxidants.

# Caraway pork with red veg

SERVES 2
PREP 15 minutes
COOK 10 minutes
CAL PER SERVE 332

**2 free-range pork chops, trimmed**
**freshly ground black pepper**
**1 teaspoon caraway seeds**
**2 teaspoons olive oil**
**1 onion, thinly sliced**
**3 garlic cloves, thinly sliced**
**300 g red cabbage, finely**
  **shredded**
**200 g fresh beetroot, peeled and**
  **cut into thin batons (see tip)**
**2 tablespoons finely chopped**
  **fresh flat-leaf parsley**

1. Season the pork with black pepper and caraway seeds.

2. Heat half the oil in a non-stick frying pan on medium–high. Cook the pork for 4 minutes each side for medium–rare or until cooked to your liking. Set aside, loosely covered with foil to keep warm.

3. Meanwhile, heat the remaining oil in a large saucepan on medium–high. Cook the onion and garlic, stirring, for 5 minutes or until soft. Stir in the cabbage and beetroot. Add ⅓ cup water and cook, covered, for 5 minutes or until the cabbage and beetroot are just tender. Season with black pepper and stir the parsley through. Serve with the pork chops.

TIP
To prepare the beetroot, use plastic gloves. Thinly slice the beetroot (using a mandoline if you have one) and then, piling up 3–4 slices at a time, thinly slice into 2 mm batons.

I'm a huge fan of stir-fries. They are quick to prepare, adaptable so you can use whatever ingredients you have on hand, and the cooking method means they are not drowning in oil. Here I've used gai lan, but you can substitute ordinary broccoli as well; just cut it up quite small so it cooks through quickly.

# Lamb & Asian greens stir-fry

SERVES 2
PREP 15 minutes
COOK 10 minutes
CAL PER SERVE 421

**75 g dried pad thai rice noodles**
**1 teaspoon peanut oil**
**250 g boneless lamb loin, trimmed and thickly sliced**
**1 bunch gai lan (Chinese broccoli), cut into chunks, leaves and stalks separated**
**100 g snow peas, halved on the diagonal**
**5 spring onions, cut into 5 cm lengths**
**3 garlic cloves, crushed**
**3 teaspoons dark soy sauce**
**3 teaspoons light soy sauce**
**1 egg**
**sliced fresh red chilli, to serve**

1. Cook the noodles in a saucepan of boiling water for 4 minutes or until tender. Drain and cool under cold running water. Drain well.

2. Meanwhile, heat the oil in a wok on high. Stir-fry the lamb, in two batches, for 2–3 minutes or until browned. Set aside.

3. Reduce the heat to medium–high. Stir-fry the gai lan stalks and snow peas for 2 minutes. Add the spring onion and stir-fry for 2 minutes. Add the garlic and stir-fry for 1 minute. Add the noodles and sauces and stir-fry until the noodles are well coated. Make a well in the centre of the mixture and crack an egg into the middle. Cook, stirring the egg, for 1 minute, then return the lamb to the wok with the gai lan leaves and stir-fry until hot and the leaves have just wilted.

TIP
When stir-frying Asian greens such as gai lan, choy sum or bok choy, separate the leaves from the stalks and only add the leaves at the end as they take no time to wilt.

VARIATION
For a vegetarian version, replace the lamb with 200 g firm tofu, cut into cubes (407 cal per serve).

One to get stuck into – in both senses of the word. It's a good dish to get the kids involved in the kitchen, rolling the meatballs. And when this hearty stew is ready to go, just watch them dive in with their forks.

# Spicy Spanish lamb meatballs

SERVES 4
PREP 20 minutes
COOK 30 minutes
CAL PER SERVE 373

300 g lean lamb mince
30 g stale breadcrumbs made
   from wholemeal bread
1 egg
½ teaspoon ground chilli
2 teaspoons smoked sweet paprika
2 teaspoons ground cumin
2 teaspoons ground coriander
3 garlic cloves, crushed
¼ cup chopped fresh
   flat-leaf parsley
freshly ground black pepper
1 tablespoon olive oil
1 brown onion, finely chopped
1 fennel bulb, trimmed
   and thinly sliced
400 g can diced **tomatoes**
400 g can **chickpeas**, drained
   and rinsed
400 g can mixed beans, drained
   and rinsed
1 tablespoon low-sodium
   tomato paste

1. Combine the mince, breadcrumbs, egg, chilli, 1 teaspoon each of paprika, cumin and coriander, the garlic and 1 tablespoon of parsley in a medium bowl. Season with black pepper. With wet hands, roll the mixture into 20 balls.

2. Heat half the oil in a large non-stick saucepan on medium–high. Cook the meatballs, turning, for 4–5 minutes or until browned. Set aside.

3. Heat the remaining oil in the same pan on medium–high. Cook the onion and fennel, stirring, for 5 minutes. Reduce the heat to low, and cook, covered, for another 5 minutes or until softened. Stir in the remaining spices and cook for 30 seconds or until fragrant. Add the tomatoes, chickpeas, beans and tomato paste. Bring to the boil. Reduce the heat and simmer, covered, for 5 minutes. Return the meatballs to the pan and simmer, covered, for 10 minutes. Stir through the remaining parsley to serve.

TIP
Freeze individual portions in airtight containers for up to one month. You could stir through 200 g baby spinach leaves at the end of cooking (387 cal per serve).

I'm always surprised when someone (apart from vegetarians, of course) tells me that they haven't eaten kangaroo: what's stopping you? It's healthy, gives you oodles of nutrients, is relatively cheap and is ethical and sustainable. The hint of gaminess goes so well here with the sweetness of the chips and the zesty orange.

# Kangaroo with sweet potato chips

1. Preheat the oven to 200°C (180°C fan-forced). Line a large baking tray with baking paper. Arrange the sweet potato in a single layer on the tray. Season with black pepper and lightly spray with oil. Roast for 45 minutes, turning halfway through.

2. Meanwhile, place the spinach leaves and the orange segments in a bowl. Combine the oil, mustard and 2 teaspoons of the reserved orange juice in a small bowl. Season with black pepper.

3. Lightly spray a medium non-stick frying pan with oil and heat on high. Season the kangaroo with black pepper and cook for 1–2 minutes each side for rare or until cooked to your liking. Set aside, loosely covered with foil, for 3 minutes to rest.

4. Drizzle the salad with the mustard dressing and gently toss to coat. Serve the kangaroo with the chips and salad alongside.

TIP
See page 28 for how to segment an orange.

SERVES 2
PREP 15 minutes
COOK 50 minutes
CAL PER SERVE 383

325 g sweet potato, peeled and cut into chips
freshly ground black pepper
olive oil spray
80 g baby **spinach** leaves
1 **orange**, segmented, juice reserved
2 teaspoons extra-virgin olive oil
1 teaspoon Dijon mustard
300 g **kangaroo** fillet, trimmed

Kangaroo? Check. Cauliflower? Check. Tomatoes? Check.
Three superfoods – one meat, one vegetable and one fruit –
make this a supremely healthy dinner. And it's so frickin' tasty!

# Kangaroo fillet with mash & tomatoes

SERVES 2
PREP 15 minutes
COOK 10 minutes
CAL PER SERVE 403

**400 g cauliflower,** cut
  into chunks
**400 g can cannellini beans,**
  drained and rinsed
**2 teaspoons olive oil**
**2 garlic cloves, thinly sliced**
**250 g vine truss cherry tomatoes**
**300 g kangaroo fillet,** trimmed
  and cut into 6 cm pieces
**2 teaspoons dried oregano**
**freshly ground black pepper**
**1 teaspoon lemon juice**

1. Steam the cauliflower for 10 minutes or until very tender. Drain, reserving 2 tablespoons of the steaming liquid. Place the cauliflower and beans into a blender. Blend until smooth, adding the reserved water until you reach the desired consistency.

2. Meanwhile, heat the oil in a medium non-stick frying pan on medium. Cook the garlic and tomatoes for 4 minutes or until the garlic is golden and the tomatoes start to blister. Remove with a slotted spoon and set aside.

3. Season the kangaroo with the oregano and black pepper. Increase the heat to high and cook the kangaroo for 1–2 minutes each side for rare or until cooked to your liking. Drizzle with the lemon juice. Set aside, loosely covered with foil, for 3 minutes to rest.

4. Serve the kangaroo with the mash, tomatoes and garlic alongside.

TIPS
Kangaroo is at its best eaten rare to medium–rare or it can become tough.

There is no fat on kangaroo fillets, but be sure to remove any nerves before cooking the meat.

I might have been a bit cheeky with this title – there's no actual rice in this dish! It is, however, an intriguingly different way to prepare cauliflower. There's heaps of other good stuff in there too, with peas and snow peas, prawns and tofu, which has lots of protein, calcium and iron.

# Cauliflower fried 'rice'

SERVES 2
PREP 20 minutes
COOK 10 minutes
CAL PER SERVE 323

**350g cauliflower,** broken
  into florets
**2 teaspoons peanut oil**
**1 egg,** lightly beaten
**500g king green prawns,**
  peeled and deveined,
  tails intact
**2 garlic cloves,** crushed
**2 spring onions,** thinly sliced
**150g firm tofu,** drained
  and cut into cubes
**½ teaspoon ground turmeric**
**½ cup (60g) frozen peas**
**100g snow peas,** trimmed
  and sliced on the diagonal
**3 teaspoons soy sauce**
**½ long fresh red chilli,**
  finely chopped

1. Process the cauliflower in batches into rice grain-sized pieces.

2. Heat ½ teaspoon of the peanut oil in a wok on high. Pour in the egg, swirling the wok to make a large omelette. Cook for 1 minute or until set. Flip onto a clean board, roll up tightly and thinly slice.

3. Heat ½ teaspoon of the peanut oil in the same wok on high. Stir-fry the prawns, garlic and half the spring onion for 3 minutes or until the prawns are pink. Set aside.

4. Heat ½ teaspoon of the peanut oil in the same wok over high heat. Stir-fry the tofu and turmeric for 1 minute or until well coated. Set aside.

5. Heat the remaining oil in the same wok on high. Stir-fry the cauliflower, peas and snow peas for 3 minutes or until hot. Return the prawns and tofu to the wok with the soy sauce and half the chilli and stir-fry until hot. Serve topped with the omelette and the remaining chilli and spring onion.

TIP
To avoid over-processing the cauliflower, do it in small batches for 5 seconds at a time. Transfer the cauliflower to a bowl and put any big pieces back into the processor.

Snapper is such a great fish. Just edged out of superhero status by salmon and sardines, it nevertheless provides a potent punch of protein, as well as all-important brain-boosting omega-3s.

# Roasted lemon & thyme snapper

SERVES 2
PREP 15 minutes
COOK 1 hour 15 minutes
CAL PER SERVE 401

olive oil spray
1 large onion, finely chopped
5 Roma **tomatoes**, diced
2 teaspoons fresh thyme leaves,
   plus 8 sprigs extra
1 tablespoon raw **wheatgerm**
freshly ground black pepper
40 g sliced sourdough, finely
   chopped
1 tablespoon olive oil
1 lemon, thinly sliced
800 g whole snapper, gutted
   and descaled

1. Preheat the oven to 180°C (160°C fan-forced).

2. Lightly spray a large non-stick frying pan with olive oil and place over medium–high heat. Cook the onion, stirring, for 5 minutes or until softened. Add the tomato, thyme leaves and wheatgerm and toss to combine. Season with black pepper and then spoon into a 3½-cup (875 ml) ovenproof dish. Toss the bread in half the oil and sprinkle over the tomato mixture. Bake for 45 minutes. Set aside, covered with foil to keep warm.

3. Increase the oven to 220°C (200°C fan-forced). Place a few slices of lemon and sprigs of thyme into the fish's cavity. Brush the fish with the remaining oil and place on top of the remaining slices of lemon and sprigs of thyme in a large roasting dish. Season with black pepper and roast for 25 minutes. Reheat the tomato and onion bake in the oven, loosely covered with foil, for the last 10 minutes of cooking time.

Pan-frying a piece of fish is a quick, healthy cooking method that keeps all the nutrients intact. The rocket adds something different to the mash, and it is relatively high in calcium, particularly for a vegetable.

# Barramundi with rocket & lemon mash

SERVES 2
PREP 10 minutes
COOK 20 minutes
CAL PER SERVE 333

300 g potatoes, peeled and
  chopped
400 g **cauliflower,** chopped
⅓ cup (80 ml) hot low-cal milk
1 bunch rocket, trimmed and
  coarsely chopped
1 teaspoon grated lemon zest
freshly ground black pepper
2 x 150 g skinless barramundi
  fillets
olive oil spray

1. Steam the potatoes over a saucepan of boiling water for 10 minutes. Add the cauliflower and steam for another 10 minutes. Place in a large bowl. Add the hot milk and coarsely mash using a potato masher. Stir the rocket and lemon zest through and season with black pepper.

2. Meanwhile, season the fish with black pepper. Lightly spray a non-stick frying pan with oil and heat over medium–high heat. Cook the fish for 3–5 minutes each side or until golden and just cooked through.

3. Serve the fish with the rocket and lemon mash alongside.

TIP
Use chopped baby rocket if you can't find a bunch of rocket.

VARIATION
Make this mash with a grilled salmon fillet and stir through 150 g baby spinach instead of rocket (396 cal per serve).

Very simple to prepare, this bake sees the potatoes take on some of the taste of the fish. You can buy fresh sardine fillets at the market or your local fishmonger. They are very inexpensive but packed with flavour and goodness.

# Sicilian sardine & potato bake

1. Place the potatoes in a saucepan and cover with water. Bring to the boil and cook for 15 minutes or until almost tender. Drain and cool slightly. When cool enough to handle, thinly slice.

2. Preheat the oven to 220°C (200°C fan-forced).

3. Arrange the potatoes, sardines and garlic in rows in two 1¼-cup shallow ovenproof dishes. Season with a pinch of cayenne. Lightly spray with oil and bake for 20 minutes or until the potatoes are tender and the sardines are cooked.

4. Meanwhile, steam the broccoli over a saucepan of boiling water for 3 minutes or until just tender. Serve the sardine bake with the broccoli and lemon wedges alongside.

TIP
Choose potatoes that will keep their shape when cooked such as desirée or kipflers.

SERVES 2
PREP 10 minutes
COOK 35 minutes
CAL PER SERVE 389

300 g desirée potatoes, peeled
200 g fresh sardine fillets
3 garlic cloves, thinly sliced
pinch cayenne pepper
olive oil spray
300 g broccoli, cut into florets
lemon wedges, to serve

A very simple but supremely tasty dish. Sardines are one of my go-to convenience foods. I keep a couple of cans in the pantry so I can quickly rustle up dinners like this, or pop them in a sandwich for lunch. Plus, their lustrous silver colour combined with the deep green broccolini and the red blush of the tomatoes makes for a tantalisingly good-looking plate of food!

# Sardine & chilli linguine

SERVES 2
PREP 10 minutes
COOK 15 minutes
CAL PER SERVE 415

**120 g dried linguine pasta**
**1 bunch broccolini, trimmed**
**and cut into chunks**
**105 g can sardines in oil,**
**drained, oil reserved**
**¼ teaspoon dried chilli flakes**
**2 garlic cloves, crushed**
**100 g grape tomatoes, halved**
**freshly ground black pepper**

1. Cook the pasta in a medium saucepan of boiling water according to the packet directions. Add the broccolini 2 minutes before the end of the cooking time. Drain and dry the pan.

2. Heat the pan on medium and add the sardines, 3 teaspoons of the reserved oil from the can, the chilli flakes and the garlic. Cook, stirring, for 1–2 minutes or until fragrant and heated through. Toss through the pasta, broccolini and tomatoes. Season with black pepper to serve.

TIP
You could also use broccoli for this recipe.

Curry? In a healthy-eating recipe book? A lot of people say that to me when they first read the title, but curries don't have to be the fat-filled, cream-soaked affairs you get from the late-night takeaway. This version keeps all the flavour, but dials back on the calories.

# Chicken curry

1. Cut the silverbeet leaves away from the stems. Thinly slice the stems and set aside. Discard the white vein from the leaves. Coarsely shred the leaves and set aside.

2. Heat the oil in a large saucepan over medium–high heat. Cook the onion and silverbeet stems, stirring occasionally, for 8 minutes. Reduce the heat to medium and cook, stirring, for another 10 minutes or until starting to brown. Stir in the garlic, ginger and spices and cook for 1 minute or until fragrant. Add the tomato and cook for 1 minute, stirring, or until the tomato starts to break down. Stir in the yoghurt and ¼ cup (60 ml) water until combined. Add the chicken and turn to coat. Bring to a simmer. Reduce the heat to low and cook, covered, for 30 minutes or until cooked through. Stir through the silverbeet leaves, in two batches, until wilted. Cook, covered, for 2 minutes or until the leaves are bright green.

3. Sprinkle with the chilli and serve with the rice alongside.

TIP
You can freeze this curry in airtight containers for up to one month.

VARIATION
Instead of serving this dish with rice, you could stir 800 g drained and rinsed canned **chickpeas** through the curry in step 2 when adding the chicken (368 cal per serve).

SERVES 6
PREP 15 minutes
COOK 55 minutes
CAL PER SERVE 387

1 bunch **silverbeet**, trimmed, washed
1 tablespoon vegetable oil
2 brown onions, thinly sliced
8 garlic cloves, crushed
1 tablespoon grated fresh ginger
1 tablespoon ground coriander
2 teaspoons ground cumin
1½ teaspoons ground turmeric
1 teaspoon fennel seeds
½ teaspoon ground cardamom
2 cinnamon sticks
2 ripe **tomatoes**, diced
1 cup (280 g) no-fat Greek-style yoghurt
875 g chicken thigh fillets, trimmed and each cut into three
1 long fresh red chilli, finely chopped
3 cups steamed basmati rice

There's a real Middle Eastern feel to this dish, with the chicken and the spices balanced by the dates. Dates are very good for you, too. They are full of fibre and are a good source of potassium, which is lost when we sweat – so good for the exercisers out there (by which I mean everyone, of course!)

# Chicken, pumpkin & date tagine

1. Heat half the oil in a large non-stick saucepan on high. Season the chicken with black pepper and cook in three batches for 4 minutes per batch or until well browned. Set aside.

2. Heat the remaining oil in the same pan on medium heat. Cook the onion, stirring, for 5 minutes or until softened. Stir in the garlic and ras el hanout and cook for 1 minute or until fragrant. Add the stock. Return the chicken to the pan with the chickpeas and the pumpkin (don't worry about the amount of stock, the pumpkin will break down and let out a lot of moisture). Bring to the boil. Reduce the heat and simmer, covered, for 20 minutes, stirring halfway through. Stir in the dates. Cook for another 10 minutes or until the chicken is cooked and the pumpkin is tender. Stir in the coriander and lemon juice.

3. Preheat the oven to 220°C (200°C fan-forced).

4. Divide the chicken mixture between six 1¼-cup (310 ml) ovenproof dishes. Stack six sheets of filo pastry, lightly spraying with oil between each layer. Roll and cut into 1 cm strips. Loosen the pastry with your fingers to disentangle it and place roughly over the chicken mixture. Bake for 12 minutes or until the filo is golden and crisp.

TIPS
You can freeze the cooled chicken tagine after step 2 in an airtight container for up to one month (370 cal without the filo topping).

Wrap the remaining filo in plastic wrap and store in the fridge.

SERVES 6
PREP 15 minutes
COOK 1 hour 10 minutes
CAL PER SERVE 410

1 tablespoon olive oil
850 g chicken thigh fillets, trimmed and cut into 3 cm cubes
freshly ground black pepper
2 onions, chopped
5 garlic cloves, crushed
1 tablespoon ras el hanout (Moroccan spice mix)
1 cup (250 ml) low-sodium chicken stock
400 g can **chickpeas**, drained and rinsed
1.2 kg pumpkin, peeled, cut into chunks
8 fresh dates, halved and deseeded
½ cup chopped fresh coriander
1 tablespoon lemon juice
6 sheets filo pastry
olive oil spray

I don't know who first thought of combining lemon and chicken, but boy, am I glad they did. So scrumptious. With brussels sprouts and tomatoes, you are getting two superfoods, but the pumpkin is also pretty handy on the health front, providing carotenoids and lots of vitamin C.

# Roast lemon chicken with vegetables

SERVES 2
PREP 15 minutes
COOK 45 minutes
CAL PER SERVE 401

330 g skinless chicken thigh
   fillets, trimmed
400 g Kent pumpkin,
   cut into wedges
150 g **brussels sprouts,**
   halved if large
200 g zucchini, cut into chunks
1 onion, unpeeled, quartered
½ lemon, halved
6 garlic cloves, unpeeled
freshly ground black pepper
1 teaspoon olive oil
100 g cherry **tomatoes**

1. Preheat the oven to 200°C (180°C fan-forced).

2. Place the chicken, pumpkin, brussels sprouts, zucchini, onion, lemon and garlic on a large baking tray in a single layer. Season with black pepper and drizzle with the oil. Toss to coat. Bake for 30 minutes, basting halfway through. Add the tomatoes and bake for 15 minutes or until the chicken is cooked through and golden.

3. Serve the chicken drizzled with the pan juices and with the vegetables alongside.

TIPS
You can easily double this recipe for guests or to have some leftover roasted chicken for sandwiches or salads.

Make sure that all the ingredients are arranged in a single layer so they roast evenly (use two trays if you haven't got a big enough tray).

I love a lasagne. Roasting the vegetables first gives them a lovely hint of sweetness that goes really well with the robust flavour of the cheese. This is a great dish to freeze for easy meals when you are in a rush.

# Roasted vegetable lasagne

SERVES 6
PREP 20 minutes
COOK 1 hour 45 minutes
CAL PER SERVE 354

**1 kg eggplant, trimmed and
cut into 3 cm chunks**
**500 g zucchini, thickly sliced**
**2 red capsicums, thickly sliced**
**5 garlic cloves, unpeeled**
**1 kg Roma tomatoes, chopped**
**4 onions, cut into wedges**
**2 teaspoons dried oregano**
**1½ tablespoons olive oil**
**⅓ cup (50 g) cornflour**
**3 cups (750 ml) low-cal milk**
**1 cup (120 g) grated low-cal
cheddar cheese**
**freshly ground black pepper**
**8 sheets (200 g) wholemeal lasagne**
**mixed salad leaves, to serve**

1. Preheat the oven to 220°C (200°C fan-forced).

2. Place the eggplant, zucchini, capsicum and garlic on two large baking trays. Place the tomatoes and onion on a third large baking tray. Sprinkle the three trays with the oregano and drizzle with the oil. Toss to coat and bake for 1 hour or until very tender and caramelised, stirring halfway through. Set aside to cool slightly.

3. Meanwhile, combine the cornflour and ½ cup of the milk in a jug. Place the remaining milk in a saucepan and bring to the boil over high heat. Whisk in the cornflour mixture and bring to the boil. Cook, stirring, for 1 minute or until the sauce thickens. Stir in half the cheese until smooth. Season with black pepper.

4. When cool enough to handle, squeeze the garlic cloves from the skins. Combine all the roasted vegetables and garlic in a bowl.

5. Reduce the oven to 200°C (180°C fan-forced). Layer a third of the vegetable mixture, pasta sheets and cheese sauce in a 24 cm square ovenproof dish. Repeat twice with the remaining vegetable mixture, pasta sheets and cheese sauce. Sprinkle with the remaining cheese. Bake for 45 minutes or until the vegetables are tender and the cheese is golden. Serve with the mixed leaves alongside.

TIP
You can freeze the cooled lasagne in airtight containers for up to one month.

Here's another way to use fruit – in this case cranberries – that you may not have thought of. The berries offer a sweet contrast to the mild spice of the turmeric and the nutty crunch of the almonds, lifting this dish from okay to awesome.

# Indian cauliflower pilaf

SERVES 2
PREP 10 minutes
COOK 30 minutes
CAL PER SERVE 404

**2 teaspoons olive oil**
**1 brown onion, finely chopped**
**½ cup (100 g) basmati rice**
**1 teaspoon ground turmeric**
**1½ tablespoons dried cranberries**
**450 g cauliflower, cut into florets**
**10 silverbeet leaves, trimmed
  and coarsely chopped**
**1½ tablespoons raw almonds,
  chopped**
**2 tablespoons chopped fresh
  coriander**

1. Heat the oil in a medium saucepan on medium. Cook the onion, stirring, for 5 minutes or until softened. Stir in the rice and turmeric until the rice is well coated. Add 1 cup (250 ml) water and the cranberries. Stir and bring to the boil. Place the cauliflower florets on top of the rice. Reduce the heat to low and cook, covered, for 13 minutes. Remove from the heat and set aside (without lifting the lid) for 10 minutes or until the rice is tender.

2. Meanwhile, steam the silverbeet leaves over a saucepan of boiling water for 2 minutes or until bright green.

3. Fluff up the rice with a fork and sprinkle with the almonds and coriander. Serve with the steamed silverbeet alongside.

TIP
Serve with ⅓ cup no-fat Greek-style yoghurt (433 cal per serve).

Barley is quite an under-used ingredient. Which is a shame, because it's super high in fibre, making it beneficial to the health of your digestive system, and selenium, which helps regulate your thyroid. Add in two superfoods – mushrooms and asparagus – and this risotto offers an easy, nutritious way to introduce barley into your cooking.

# Barley & mushroom risotto

**1.** Heat half the oil in a medium saucepan on medium. Cook the onion, stirring, for 5 minutes or until softened. Stir in the barley, stock and 1¼ cups (310 ml) water. Bring to the boil. Reduce the heat to low and simmer, covered, for 25 minutes. Remove the lid and cook, uncovered, for another 10–15 minutes or until the barley is tender and the liquid is absorbed.

**2.** Meanwhile, heat the remaining oil in a large frying pan over high heat. Cook the mushrooms, stirring, for 6 minutes or until golden and tender. Stir in the garlic and parsley and cook for 1 minute or until fragrant.

**3.** Cook the asparagus in a saucepan of boiling water for 2 minutes or until just tender. Drain.

**4.** Stir the mushroom mixture, asparagus and parmesan through the barley and season with black pepper.

SERVES 2
PREP 10 minutes
COOK 45 minutes
CAL PER SERVE 393

**2 teaspoons olive oil**
**1 small brown onion, finely chopped**
**¾ cup (150 g) pearl barley**
**1 cup (250 ml) low-sodium vegetable stock**
**200 g button mushrooms, quartered**
**2 garlic cloves, crushed**
**2 tablespoons coarsely chopped fresh flat-leaf parsley**
**1 bunch asparagus, trimmed and cut into chunks**
**2 tablespoons grated parmesan cheese**
**freshly ground black pepper**

After the initial prep, this dish sits in the oven, filling your kitchen with wonderful aromas. All the flavours combine to delicious effect. I serve it with broccoli as a side because it's a superfood . . . and I love it . . . but you can use other veg as an accompaniment if you prefer, such as green beans.

# Slow-cooked lamb shanks

SERVES 6
PREP 15 minutes
COOK 2 hours 35 minutes
CAL PER SERVE 383

**6 lamb shanks, trimmed**
**freshly ground black pepper**
**2 teaspoons olive oil**
**1 onion, chopped**
**1 carrot, diced**
**1 celery stalk, diced**
**4 garlic cloves, thinly sliced**
**6 sprigs fresh thyme**
**1 bay leaf**
**1½ cups (325 ml) low-sodium**
  **beef stock**
**½ cup (125 ml) red wine**
**2 tablespoons low-sodium**
  **tomato paste**
**1.8 kg celeriac, peeled**
  **and cut into chunks**
**600 g broccoli**

1. Preheat the oven to 180°C (160°C fan-forced).

2. Season the lamb with black pepper. Heat half the oil in a large saucepan on medium–high. Cook the lamb in two batches for 5 minutes or until browned all over. Set aside.

3. Heat the remaining oil in the pan on medium. Cook the onion, carrot, celery, garlic, thyme and bay leaf, stirring, for 8–10 minutes or until the vegetables are softened.

4. Meanwhile, whisk the stock, wine and tomato paste in a jug until combined. Return the lamb to the pan with the stock mixture and bring to the boil. Cook, covered, in the oven for 2 hours, turning the shanks twice, until the meat is very tender. Set the shanks aside. Bring the sauce to the boil. Reduce the heat to medium and simmer for 15 minutes or until thickened. Remove from the heat and stand for 5 minutes to let any fat settle at the surface. Use a spoon to de-grease the sauce.

5. Return the shanks to the pan and cook for 1–2 minutes or until hot.

6. Meanwhile, steam the celeriac over a saucepan of boiling water for 15 minutes or until very tender. Drain well and process until smooth. Season with black pepper.

7. Steam the broccoli over a saucepan of boiling water for 5 minutes or until just tender. Serve the lamb shanks with the celeriac mash and broccoli alongside.

TIPS
You can freeze the cooled stew in airtight containers for up to one month (297 cal without the mash and broccoli).

You can make the stew in advance up to step 4 (the flavours will develop and it will be a cinch to de-grease the sauce once it's cooled in the fridge).

This quick-and-easy stir-fry packs a lot in, nutrient-wise. You might think that it sounds like a lot of garlic, but the flavour mellows as it cooks and is balanced with the sweetness of the oyster sauce. And, anyway, garlic is a useful ingredient for your health as well, helping to keep your blood in fine fettle.

# Kale, mushroom & cashew stir-fry

SERVES 2
PREP 10 minutes
COOK 20 minutes
CAL PER SERVE 393

⅓ cup chopped cashews
1 teaspoon peanut oil
500 g mixed **mushrooms**, chopped if very large
4 garlic cloves, crushed
1 bunch **kale**, trimmed and coarsely shredded
1 tablespoon oyster sauce
1 cup steamed basmati rice, to serve

1. Heat a wok on medium–high. Stir-fry the cashews for 3–4 minutes or until toasted. Set aside.

2. Heat the oil in the wok on high. Stir-fry the mushrooms in three batches for 3–4 minutes or until golden. Add the garlic to the last batch and stir-fry for 30 seconds or until fragrant. Set aside.

3. Add the kale to the wok and stir-fry for 1 minute or until bright green and starting to wilt (add a few splashes of water if the kale starts to stick to the wok). Return the mushrooms to the wok with the oyster sauce and the cashews and stir-fry for 1 minute or until hot. Serve with the rice.

TIPS
I use a combination of shiitake, swiss brown and oyster mushrooms.

To prepare the kale, discard the stems and wash well to remove any grit.

Cook the pasta. Sauté the veg. Combine and top with cheese. With ingredients this good, you don't need to do more. Simple as 1, 2, 3. Tasty as anything.

# Kale & tomato pasta

SERVES 2
PREP 10 minutes
COOK 15 minutes
CAL PER SERVE 392

**120 g wholemeal pasta**
**2 teaspoons extra-virgin olive oil**
**1 bunch kale, trimmed and**
   **coarsely shredded**
**200 g cherry tomatoes, halved**
**3 garlic cloves, crushed**
**½ cup (120 g) fresh low-cal**
   **ricotta cheese, crumbled**
**freshly ground black pepper**

1. Cook the pasta in a saucepan of boiling water according to the packet directions. Drain. Return the pasta to the pan.

2. Meanwhile, heat the oil in a large frying pan over medium–high heat. Cook the kale, stirring, for 1 minute or until wilted. Stir in the tomatoes and garlic and cook for 2 minutes.

3. Toss the kale mixture through the pasta. Serve sprinkled with ricotta and then season with black pepper.

TIPS

You could use silverbeet or spinach leaves instead of kale.

I like to use fresh ricotta but you can use ricotta sold in packets. It's slightly wetter so use a small spoon to add dollops to the pasta.

A risotto is the type of dish that really rewards your efforts. You have to put in the time at the stove to achieve the right consistency, but it is so worth it. The cooking time allows the flavours to deepen and fuse together perfectly. A handful of spinach leaves adds a finishing touch and ups the nutritional ante.

# Beetroot risotto

1. Bring the stock and 2 cups (500 ml) water to a simmer in a saucepan on medium.

2. Heat the oil in a large saucepan over medium heat. Cook the onion, stirring, for 5 minutes or until softened. Stir in the rice and beetroot. Cook for another minute. Add a ladle of the simmering stock mixture. Cook on medium, stirring until the stock is absorbed. Continue adding the remaining stock a ladleful at a time, stirring constantly until each is absorbed (it will take about 25 minutes for the rice to become tender).

3. Remove from the heat. Stir the parmesan through and then set aside, covered, for 5 minutes. Season with black pepper. Serve with the spinach leaves alongside.

TIP
If you're not a fan of green leaves, stir the spinach through the risotto instead.

SERVES 2
PREP 15 minutes
COOK 35 minutes
CAL PER SERVE 395

1 cup (250 ml) reduced-salt
   vegetable stock
1 tablespoon olive oil
1 onion, finely chopped
½ cup (100 g) arborio rice
300 g **beetroot**, peeled
   and coarsely grated
¼ cup grated parmesan cheese
freshly ground black pepper
80 g baby **spinach** leaves, to serve

Cauliflower and cheese – what a flavourful combination.
With the addition of broccoli, you get a double whammy of
cruciferous goodness as well. The cheese provides protein
and calcium, but use a low-calorie version to avoid too much fat.

# Cauliflower & broccoli cheese

SERVES 2
PREP 10 minutes
COOK 45 minutes
CAL PER SERVE 388

**700 g cauliflower, trimmed
and broken into large florets**
**1 large head broccoli (300 g),
trimmed and broken
into large florets**
**2½ tablespoons cornflour**
**2 cups (500 ml) low-cal milk**
**1 cup (120 g) grated low-cal
cheddar cheese**
**freshly ground black pepper**
**pinch freshly grated nutmeg**
**pinch cayenne pepper**
**mixed salad leaves, to serve**

1. Preheat the oven to 200°C (180°C fan-forced).

2. Steam the cauliflower over a large saucepan of boiling water for 4 minutes.
Add the broccoli and steam for another 4 minutes or until just tender. Place in
a 5-cup (1.25 L) capacity ovenproof dish.

3. Meanwhile, combine the cornflour and ¼ cup milk in a jug. Place the
remaining milk in a saucepan and bring to the boil over high heat. Whisk in
the cornflour mixture and cook, stirring, for 2–3 minutes or until the sauce boils
and thickens. Stir in half the cheese until smooth. Season with black pepper and
nutmeg. Pour over the cauliflower and broccoli. Sprinkle with the remaining
cheese and cayenne. Bake for 30 minutes or until bubbly and golden.

4. Serve with the salad leaves alongside.

Desserts always seem like a rare treat. Usually, that's because they are full of sugar and calories. But there is another way. The dessert ideas below are good for you – packed with superfood nutrients and low in calories – and taste like treats too! All of the methods are for a single serving, but are so simple that they can easily be scaled up for two, for the whole family, or even more for a party.

# Desserts

## Grilled bananas with blueberries & passionfruit

Halve a banana lengthways and chargrill for 30 seconds each side until lightly charred and warm. Serve with a dollop of no-fat Greek-style **yoghurt**, a handful of **blueberries** and the pulp of 1 passionfruit. Around 108 calories.

## Mixed berry sorbet

Process 1 large frozen banana until smooth. Add 150 g frozen mixed **berries** and process until smooth. Serve a scoop and freeze the remaining sorbet in an airtight container for up to one month. Around 36 calories per scoop.

## Raspberry fool

Whisk together ¼ cup each of smooth low-cal ricotta cheese and low-cal vanilla **yoghurt** until smooth. Layer fresh or thawed frozen **raspberries** in a serving glass with the ricotta mixture to form several layers. Sprinkle with 1 teaspoon toasted flaked almonds. Around 183 calories.

## The ultra superfood fruit salad

Combine half a thinly sliced red **apple**, 1 chopped **kiwifruit**, a handful of fresh **blueberries**, 1 tablespoon dried **cranberries**, 1 tablespoon **orange** juice and 2 teaspoons torn mint leaves. Around 154 calories.

# Crepes suzette style

Bring 2 tablespoons of **orange** juice to the boil in a small pan and reduce by half. Remove from the heat. Dip 1 thawed frozen crepe into the syrup and transfer to a serving plate. Top with **orange** segments. Around 183 calories.

# Stewed apple & strawberries with honey yoghurt

Peel and chop a red **apple**. Cook with 1 tablespoon water in a small saucepan until the apple is soft but still holds its shape. Stir through 100 g chopped strawberries and cook for 30 seconds. Serve warm with 2 tablespoons no-fat Greek-style **yoghurt** drizzled with 1 teaspoon honey. Around 185 calories.

# Orange & blueberry popsicles

Whisk 1 cup **orange** juice and ½ cup no-fat Greek-style **yoghurt** until smooth. Stir through a handful of fresh **blueberries** and pour into small ice popsicle moulds. Freeze until firm. Around 52 calories per popsicle.

# Mango & raspberry frozen yoghurt

Purée half a mango and chop remaining half. Purée and strain 150 g **raspberries**. Combine puréed and chopped mango with ½ cup low-cal vanilla **yoghurt** and fill small popsicle moulds halfway up. Freeze until firm. Combine the strained raspberry purée, 100 g raspberries and ½ cup low-cal vanilla yoghurt. Divide between the moulds. Freeze until firm. Around 66 calories per popsicle.

Let's put it out there, straight away – you don't have to eat snacks if you don't feel the need. You can just have slightly larger meals instead to make up your daily calorie quota. And, a lot of people find the routine of three meals a day a good way to help them control their eating. After all, a lot of the time we just eat snacks out of habit or boredom.

There are, however, times when a snack is necessary. When you're rushing around all day or have had a lighter breakfast or lunch, say. But all too often we reach for the high-calorie, sugar-laden packaged snacks that offer only a temporary lift before the inevitable crash. You can, however, snack healthily and stick to your diet program. And if you can get some superfood goodness in there as well, so much the better. Here are a few suggestions.

# Snacks

- A medium banana or apple. Around 75 calories.

- A small tub of low-cal yoghurt. Around 81 calories.

- 2 celery stalks dipped into 2 tablespoons of hummus. Around 100 calories.

- 2 large iceberg lettuce leaves filled with half a cup of leftover cooked chicken and 1 tablespoon of tomato salsa. Around 150 calories.

- 1 cup of frozen mixed berries, 3 tablespoons of low-cal yoghurt and 4 ice cubes blended together. Around 140 calories.

- 3 large slices of tomato, each topped with a slice of bocconcini cheese and a large basil leaf. Around 71 calories.

- Mix one cup of fresh strawberries and half a cup of fresh blueberries with a dollop of low-cal yoghurt. Around 99 calories.

# *SUPER*foods menu plans

Use the menu plans and shopping lists for a fuss-free approach to eating, but, of course, you can change them to suit your tastes and lifestyle. Just keep track of your calories.

The plans set out here offer a diverse menu, with lots of flavours, textures and superfood goodness. But, remember, they are just suggestions. You can, of course, follow them to the letter and you'll get a wonderfully fulfilling and healthy diet, but equally, feel free to mix them up a bit.

**All the recipes in the book have their calorie content listed, so you can keep track of your intake and eat with your goals in mind.** If you are looking to lose weight, a woman should be taking in around 1200 calories a day and a man around 1500. If you are just looking to maintain your weight, the figures are approximately 1500 for girls and 1800 for boys. The three meals in the daily plans here are typically in the range of 900–1100 calories. I've worked to 1500 calories in total so you have some flexibility. **You can eat slightly larger versions of some dishes, have a snack or finish dinner with a dessert – change the plans around to find what works for you, depending on your goals.** For instance, the breakfasts change each day, but you might find your schedule means making up a big batch of muesli and having that at the start of each weekday is best for you. Or perhaps you'll find it easier to scale up a dish at the weekend and freeze it for use during the week. **Just do a bit of meal planning, keep an eye on your calorie count, and above all . . . enjoy your food!**

# Pantry list

These are the basics to keep in your kitchen, fridge, pantry and freezer. They all keep for a reasonably long time, meaning you don't have to shop for them every week.

balsamic vinegar

bran

bread: baguette, Lebanese, rye, sourdough, Turkish, wholegrain, wholegrain & oats, rye, sourdough, wholemeal buns

brown sugar

canned beans: cannellini, **chickpeas**, mixed, red kidney

canned fish: anchovies, **sardines**

canned vegetables: **beetroot**, **tomatoes**

chilli sauce

cornflour

Dijon mustard

dried fruit: **cranberries**, mango

dried pasta: linguine, wholemeal, wholemeal lasagne sheets

**eggs**

fish sauce

frozen mixed **berries**

frozen peas

garlic

ginger, fresh

herbs and spices: caraway seeds cayenne pepper, chilli flakes, Chinese five-spice, cinnamon (ground and sticks), dried oregano, dukkah, fennel seeds, ground cardamom, ground chilli, ground coriander, ground cumin, ground turmeric, nutmeg, paprika, ras el hanout, star anise, sumac, za'atar

honey

horseradish cream

lemons

milk, low-cal

nuts: **almonds**, cashews, macadamia, pine nuts, pistachios, **walnuts**

**oats**, rolled

olive oil and olive oil spray

onions: brown, red

peanut oil

quinoa: red, white

red-wine vinegar

rice-wine vinegar

rice: arborio, basmati, brown, jasmine, white

sauces; chilli, hoisin, mirin, oyster, shaoxing, soy (dark and light)

sesame oil

stock: beef (low-sodium), chicken (low-sodium), vegetable (low-sodium)

tomato paste (low-sodium)

white-wine vinegar

# week 1 shopping list

Remember, if you're looking to lose weight it's 1200 calories per day for women and 1500 for men. To maintain your weight, the figures are 1500 calories for the girls and 1800 for the boys.

**apples**, Red Delicious
**asparagus**
baby capers
barramundi, fillets
basil
beans, green
beans, snake
beef: gravy, rump steak
**beetroot**
**blueberries**
**broccoli**
**brussels sprouts**
**cabbage**: green, red
capsicum: green, red
carrot
**cauliflower**
celeriac
celery
cheddar cheese, low-cal
**chia seeds**
chicken: sausages, whole
coriander
corn, baby
cottage cheese, low-cal
cream, light thickened
crumpets, wholemeal
cucumber, Lebanese
eggplant
fennel
**flaxseed**
**gai lan (Chinese broccoli)**
grapefruit, ruby

herring, marinated
**kiwifruit**
lamb shanks
mango
mint
**mushrooms**: field, mixed, shiitake
**oranges**
parsley, flat-leaf
parsnip
potatoes, desirée
pumpkin
radish
ricotta cheese
rocket
salad leaves
scallops, fresh
shallot
**silverbeet**
snapper, whole
snow peas
**spinach**
spring onions
strawberries
thyme
tofu, firm
**tomatoes**: grape, Roma
turnip
**watercress**
**wheatgerm**
wine, red
**yoghurt**: Greek-style, natural

# menu

| | breakfast | lunch | dinner | total cals |
|---|---|---|---|---|
| monday | Sweet quinoa tabbouleh, p. 28 **310 cal** | Spicy eggplant sandwich, p. 49 **330 cal** | Chinese soy chicken, p. 100 **387 cal** | **1027** **+ 473** cal for snacks/ desserts |
| tuesday | Oeuf cocotte, p. 38 **350 cal** | Asian chicken coleslaw, p. 78 **313 cal** | Cauliflower & broccoli cheese, p. 142 **388 cal** | **1051** **+ 449** cal for snacks/ desserts |
| wednesday | Oat porridge with apple & walnuts, p. 30 **402 cal** | Herring on rye, p. 47 **303 cal** | Chunky chili con carne, p. 108 **364 cal** | **1069** **+ 431** cal for snacks/ desserts |
| thursday | Fruit & ricotta crumpets, p. 31 **310 cal** | Tofu stir-fry, p. 65 **304 cal** | Roasted lemon & thyme snapper, p. 122 **401 cal** | **1015** **+ 485** cal for snacks/ desserts |
| friday | Super muesli, p. 24 **392 cal** | Chinese beef skewers, p. 80 **362 cal** | Root vegetable soup, p. 96 **321 cal** | **1075** **+ 425** cal for snacks/ desserts |
| saturday | Spicy mushrooms on cheesy toast, p. 32 **386 cal** | Pumpkin & tomato pide, p. 92 **328 cal** | Barramundi with rocket & lemon mash, p. 124 **333 cal** | **1047** **+ 453** cal for snacks/ desserts |
| sunday | Breakfast grill, p. 39 **333 cal** | Scallop & grapefruit salad, p. 56 **356 cal** | Slow-cooked lamb shanks, p. 136 **383 cal** | **1072** **+ 428** cal for snacks/ desserts |

# week 2 shopping list

Remember, if you're looking to lose weight it's 1200 calories per day for women and 1500 for men. To maintain your weight, the figures are 1500 calories for the girls and 1800 for the boys.

**almonds**
**asparagus**
avocado
barley, pearl
basil
basil, Thai
beef: roast, scotch fillet
**broccoli**
**calves' liver**
capsicum: red, yellow
cheddar cheese, low-cal
**chia seeds**, white
chicken, thigh fillets
chilli, fresh red
chives
coriander
cucumber, Lebanese
dill
eggplant
fennel
fetta cheese
**flaxseed**
**goji berries**
grapefruit: ruby, white
grapes, red seedless
**kale**
**kangaroo**, fillet
**kiwifruit**

lime
mango
mint
muffins, wholemeal
**mushrooms**, button
**oranges**
parmesan cheese
parsley, flat-leaf
passionfruit
pineapple
prawns
prawns, king
rice paper sheets
rice vermicelli noodles
ricotta cheese, low-cal
rockmelon
salad leaves
**silverbeet**
smoked **salmon**
**spinach**, baby
sweet potato
tofu: firm, silken firm
**tomatoes**: cherry, Roma
turkey, sliced
**watercress**
wheat biscuits
**yoghurt**, Greek-style
zucchini

# menu

| | breakfast | lunch | dinner | total cals |
|---|---|---|---|---|
| monday | Bran & citrus brekkie, p. 26 **408 cal** | Salmon & cucumber rice paper rolls, p. 44 **315 cal** | Barley & mushroom risotto, p. 135 **393 cal** | **1116** + **384 cal for snacks/ desserts** |
| tuesday | Green smoothie, p. 20 **180 cal** | Kale frittata, p. 54 **307 cal** | Kangaroo with sweet potato chips, p. 117 **383 cal** | **870** + **630 cal for snacks/ desserts** |
| wednesday | Fruit & nut wheat biscuits, p. 22 **400 cal** | Beetroot & smoked salmon sandwich, p. 46 **342 cal** | Chicken curry, p. 127 **387 cal** | **1129** + **371 cal for snacks/ desserts** |
| thursday | Quinoa bircher muesli, p. 27 **408 cal** | Chilli garlic prawns, p. 86 **299 cal** | Calves' liver with sweet potato bake, p. 106 **407 cal** | **1114** + **386 cal for snacks/ desserts** |
| friday | Moroccan eggs, p. 34 **373 cal** | Rare roast beef & pesto bun, p. 84 **304 cal** | Kale & tomato pasta, p. 140 **392 cal** | **1069** + **431 cal for snacks/ desserts** |
| saturday | Avocado, salmon & poached egg, p. 36 **363 cal** | Minted brown rice salad, p. 68 **370 cal** | Roasted vegetable lasagne, p. 132 **354 cal** | **1087** + **413 cal for snacks/ desserts** |
| sunday | Turkey & cheese toastie, p. 40 **385 cal** | Prawn, chickpea & fennel soup, p. 62 **363 cal** | Grilled steak with pineapple salad, p. 104 **311 cal** | **1059** + **441 cal for snacks/ desserts** |

# week 3 shopping list

Remember, if you're looking to lose weight it's 1200 calories per day for women and 1500 for men. To maintain your weight, the figures are 1500 calories for the girls and 1800 for the boys.

**apples**: Pink Lady, Red Delicious
**asparagus**
avocado
basil
beef, mince
**beetroot**: fresh, relish
**blueberries**
bocconcini cheese
**broccoli**
**broccolini**
**brussels sprouts**
**cauliflowe**r
celery
cheddar cheese, low-cal
**chia seeds**, white
chicken: breast, sausages, thigh fillets
chilli, red
chives
coriander
cream, light thickened
crumpets, wholemeal
dates
endive
fennel
filo pastry
**flaxseed**
goat's cheese
**kangaroo**, fillet
**kiwifruit**

lamb, mince
mango
muffin, wholemeal
**mushrooms**, field
**oranges**
parsley, flat-leaf
potatoes: carisma, desirée, sweet, white
prawns, king
pumpkin
**raspberries**
ricotta cheese, low-cal
rocket
salad leaves
**sardines**, fillets
smoked **salmon**
snow peas
**spinach**, baby
spring onions
strawberries
tarragon
thyme
tofu, firm
**tomatoes**: cherry, Roma
**watercress**
**wheatgerm**
**yoghurt**: Greek-style, natural
zucchini

# menu

| | breakfast | lunch | dinner | total cals |
|---|---|---|---|---|
| monday | Super muesli, p. 24<br>**392 cal** | Italian toasted sardine sandwich, p. 48<br>**363 cal** | Roast lemon chicken with vegetables, p. 130<br>**401 cal** | **1156**<br>**+ 344**<br>**cal for**<br>**snacks/**<br>**desserts** |
| tuesday | Oeuf cocotte, p. 38<br>**350 cal** | Chicken & horseradish roll, p. 50<br>**355 cal** | Cauliflower fried 'rice', p. 120<br>**323 cal** | **1028**<br>**+ 472**<br>**cal for**<br>**snacks/**<br>**desserts** |
| wednesday | Oat porridge with apple & walnuts, p. 30<br>**402 cal** | Hot-smoked salmon salad, p. 88<br>**372 cal** | Spicy Spanish lamb meatballs, p. 116<br>**373 cal** | **1147**<br>**+ 353**<br>**cal for**<br>**snacks/**<br>**desserts** |
| thursday | Fruit & ricotta crumpets, p. 31<br>**310 cal** | Kangaroo, fennel & broccolini stir-fry, p. 66<br>**349 cal** | Chicken, pumpkin & date tagine, p. 128<br>**410 cal** | **1069**<br>**+ 431**<br>**cal for**<br>**snacks/**<br>**desserts** |
| friday | Sweet quinoa tabbouleh, p. 28<br>**310 cal** | Tarragon chicken & potato salad, p. 74<br>**380 cal** | Sicilian sardine & potato bake, p. 125<br>**389 cal** | **1079**<br>**+ 421**<br>**cal for**<br>**snacks/**<br>**desserts** |
| saturday | Breakfast grill, p. 39<br>**333 cal** | Chickpea, pumpkin & cheese salad, p. 70<br>**348 cal** | Open beef burger with beetroot relish, p. 110<br>**405 cal** | **1086**<br>**+ 414**<br>**cal for**<br>**snacks/**<br>**desserts** |
| sunday | Avocado, salmon & poached egg, p. 36<br>**363 cal** | Roasted beetroot salad, p. 72<br>**341 cal** | Kangaroo fillet with mash & tomatoes, p. 118<br>**403 cal** | **1107**<br>**+ 393**<br>**cal for**<br>**snacks/**<br>**desserts** |

# week 4 shopping list

Remember, if you're looking to lose weight it's 1200 calories per day for women and 1500 for men. To maintain your weight, the figures are 1500 calories for the girls and 1800 for the boys.

**apples**, Red Delicious
**asparagus**
beans, green
beef
**beetroot**
**broccolini**
**brussels sprouts**
**cabbage**: green, red
**calves' liver**
capsicum: red, yellow
carrots, baby
**cauliflower**
cheddar cheese, low-cal
**chia seeds**, white
chicken, breast
chilli, red
coriander
cottage cheese, low-cal
dill
fennel
fetta cheese, low-cal
filo pastry
**flaxseed**
**goji berries**
grapefruit: white, ruby
grapes, red seedless

**kale**
**kangaroo**, fillet
**kiwifruit**
lamb, cutlets
mango
mint
**mushrooms**: button, mixed
**oranges**
parmesan cheese
passionfruit
pork, chops
rockmelon
salad leaves
**silverbeet**
snow peas
soba noodles
**spinach**
spring onion
thyme
tofu, silken firm
**tomatoes**
tuna
turkey, sliced
wheat biscuits
**yoghurt**, Greek-style

# menu

| | breakfast | lunch | dinner | total cals |
|---|---|---|---|---|
| monday | Berry smoothie, p. 20 **174 cal** | Spicy kangaroo salad with chickpeas, p. 76 **376 cal** | Indian cauliflower pilaf, p. 134 **404 cal** | **954** **+ 546 cal for snacks/ desserts** |
| tuesday | Bran & citrus brekkie, p. 26 **408 cal** | Beetroot, fetta & dill frittata, p. 52 **348 cal** | Express beef & calves' liver pie, p. 103 **366 cal** | **1122** **+ 378 cal for snacks/ desserts** |
| wednesday | Fruit & nut wheat biscuits, p. 22 **400 cal** | Tuna & fennel salad, p. 55 **382 cal** | Kale, mushroom & cashew stir-fry, p. 138 **393 cal** | **1175** **+ 425 cal for snacks/ desserts** |
| thursday | Moroccan eggs, p. 34 **373 cal** | Lebanese yoghurt & chickpea soup, p. 61 **405 cal** | Sardine & chilli linguine, p. 126 **415 cal** | **1193** **+ 307 cal for snacks/ desserts** |
| friday | Quinoa bircher muesli, p. 27 **408 cal** | Beef, sprouts & silverbeet stir-fry, p. 67 **366 cal** | Chicken salad with peas & beans, p. 98 **380 cal** | **1154** **+ 346 cal for snacks/ desserts** |
| saturday | Turkey & cheese toastie, p. 40 **385 cal** | Lamb cutlets with spring vegetables, p. 83 **380 cal** | Beetroot risotto, p. 141 **395 cal** | **1160** **+ 340 cal for snacks/ desserts** |
| sunday | Spicy mushrooms on cheesy toast, p. 32 **386 cal** | Grilled tuna with soba noodle salad, p. 90 **396 cal** | Caraway pork with red veg, p. 112 **332 cal** | **1114** **+ 386 cal for snacks/ desserts** |

# Index

Which superhero
of the food world
will you choose
today?